Editor-in-Chief and Founder:
Lyndon H. LaRouche, Jr.
Editorial Board: *Lyndon H. LaRouche, Jr. , Helga Zepp-LaRouche, Paul Gallagher, Tony Papert, Gerald Rose, Dennis Small, Jeffrey Steinberg, William Wertz*
Co-Editors: *Paul Gallagher, Tony Papert*
Managing Editor: *Nancy Spannaus*
Technology: *Marsha Freeman*
Books: *Katherine Notley*
Ebooks: *Richard Burden*
Graphics: *Alan Yue*
Photos: *Stuart Lewis*
Circulation Manager: *Stanley Ezrol*

INTELLIGENCE DIRECTORS
Counterintelligence: *Jeffrey Steinberg, Michele Steinberg*
Economics: *John Hoefle, Marcia Merry Baker, Paul Gallagher*
History: *Anton Chaitkin*
Ibero-America: *Dennis Small*
Russia and Eastern Europe: *Rachel Douglas*
United States: *Debra Freeman*

INTERNATIONAL BUREAUS
Bogotá: *Miriam Redondo*
Berlin: *Rainer Apel*
Copenhagen: *Tom Gillesberg*
Houston: *Harley Schlanger*
Lima: *Sara Madueño*
Melbourne: *Robert Barwick*
Mexico City: *Gerardo Castilleja Chávez*
New Delhi: *Ramtanu Maitra*
Paris: *Christine Bierre*
Stockholm: *Ulf Sandmark*
United Nations, N.Y.C.: *Leni Rubinstein*
Washington, D.C.: *William Jones*
Wiesbaden: *Göran Haglund*

ON THE WEB
e-mail: eirns@larouchepub.com
www.larouchepub.com
www.executiveintelligencereview.com
www.larouchepub.com/eiw
Webmaster: *John Sigerson*
Assistant Webmaster: *George Hollis*
Editor, Arabic-language edition: *Hussein Askary*

EIR (ISSN 0273-6314) *is published weekly (50 issues), by EIR News Service, Inc., P.O. Box 17390, Washington, D.C. 20041-0390. (703) 777-9451*

European Headquarters: E.I.R. GmbH, Postfach Bahnstrasse 9a, D-65205, Wiesbaden, Germany Tel: 49-611-73650
Homepage: http://www.eirna.com
e-mail: eirna@eirna.com
Director: Georg Neudecker

Montreal, Canada: 514-461-1557

Denmark: EIR - Danmark, Sankt Knuds Vej 11, basement left, DK-1903 Frederiksberg, Denmark. Tel.: +45 35 43 60 40, Fax: +45 35 43 87 57. e-mail: eirdk@hotmail.com.

Mexico City: EIR, Sor Juana Inés de la Cruz 242-2 Col. Agricultura C.P. 11360 Delegación M. Hidalgo, México D.F. Tel. (5525) 5318-2301
eirmexico@gmail.com

Canada Post Publication Sales Agreement #40683579

Postmaster: Send all address changes to *EIR*, P.O. Box 17390, Washington, D.C. 20041-0390.

Signed articles in *EIR* represent the views of the authors, and not necessarily those of the Editorial Board.

Putin Turns the Flank

EIR Contents

www.larouchepub.com Volume 42, Number 36, September 11, 2015

©TVA

Cover This Week

Russian President Putin and Chinese President Xi Jinping oversee the Sept. 3 Victory over Fascism parade in Beijing.

'Our Future Is Hanging by The Thinnest of Threads'

The following is the transcript of the Sept. 4 LaRouche PAC webcast.

Matthew Ogden: Good evening. It's Sept. 4, 2015. My name is Matthew Ogden, and I'd like to welcome you to our webcast here from larouchepac.com. I am joined in the studio tonight by both Jeffrey Steinberg and Megan Beets. Jeffrey Steinberg obviously is a representative from *Executive Intelligence Review*, and Megan Beets is joining us from the LaRouche PAC Basement Scientific team.

We had a chance to meet with both Lyndon LaRouche and Helga LaRouche literally less than an hour ago.

Now I have to say that tonight's webcast is being prerecorded; and I have to make that remark here in the beginning, to preface what's about to be said, because the situation is so quickly changing, and a rapidly changing situation is actually the substance of the subject matter of our discussion here tonight.

Mr. LaRouche's emphasis in our discussion with him earlier, was that it must be emphasized that the world is hanging in a state of suspense, and that it is very difficult to say one minute to the next, what *is* about to occur, but the situation strategically is very clear: The world is in a posture of general war, even if general war has not yet broken out, and the opportunity for a strategic game-changer,—an intervention by Russian President Vladimir Putin, especially having to do with the situation in Syria currently,—could

kremlin.ru

The targets: Chinese President Xi Jinping (to Putin's right) and Russian President Vladimir Putin (center) head to the site of Chna's 70th anniversary celebration of the end of World War II in Asia on Sept. 3.

change everything about the current world strategic situation.

Now, the opportunity for this kind of flank,—of which there are indications President Vladimir Putin is strongly considering something along these lines—is the substance of the discussion that we had with Mr. LaRouche.

You could also see on the front page of the LaRouche PAC website a statement that was published by Mr. LaRouche on Sept. 3 called, "Putin Can Change the Game with Syria Intervention." Now, I know this is in discussion among very top levels of the United States senior intelligence, and military-strategic community, and this is part of the discussion which Mr. Jeffrey Steinberg has personally been a part of.

It is the brutality of ISIS which Syrian refugees are fleeing. Here, an ISIS member prepares to behead an unknown man outside its Raqqa stronghold.

So, I'm going to hand the podium over to Jeff, to give him an opportunity to elaborate on this suspenseful situation for you right now.

I. Putin Can Change the Game

Jeffrey Steinberg: Thanks, Matt. Some of you may be aware, as of today, that for the past 48 hours, a series of news reports have been published, initially in the Israeli and Syrian media, and then picked up here in the United States, and in Europe, suggesting that Russian President Putin is about to make a strategic intervention into the crisis in Syria.

Just to situate that particular aspect of the global situation more broadly, let's just start with some very clear facts that are well-known to Mr. Putin, are well-known to Chinese President Xi Jinping, and many other world leaders: namely, that the posture of the Obama White House—and I say Obama White House as distinct from the viewpoints in some sections of the U.S. Pentagon, the Joint Chiefs of Staff, the military establishment, and some people in our diplomatic and intelligence community—the posture of the Obama White House is for a confrontation with Russia, full-scale general war confrontation with Russia, unless Russia were to back down in some kind of embarrassing and very self-destructive way.

You have the situation in Ukraine, which has been one of the frontline situations for provocation against Russia. That's been the case going all the way back to November of 2013, when Color Revolution number 2 in Ukraine was launched, and led ultimately in February of 2014 to the removal of the Yanukovych government. That was followed by the installation of a government in Kiev that is dominated, militarily speaking, by a Right-Sector apparatus that is the direct continuity of the wartime allies of Hitler and the Nazis within Ukraine, namely the movement of Stepan Bandera and others.

So, Ukraine has been a frontline situation in this. You've had two other situations that, during the same timeframe, even going back to 2011, have emerged as critical areas where the ultimate targets have been Russia and China.

The first of these is Libya, where the U.S.-Obama-led, with allied support from France and Britain, overthrow and execution of the Qaddafi government has created a major crisis that has spread out from Libya across all of North Africa, and extending further south, so that the whole African continent has been destabilized as a result of the overthrow of Qaddafi, and the unleashing of jihadist forces with enormous supplies of weapons. You've had an ongoing situation in the case of Libya, where various Saudi- and British-backed jihadist elements have been largely in control of the country. You've got now, at this point, an official branch of the Islamic State operating inside Libya under one of the leading jihadists in the overthrow of Qaddafi, a man named Belhadj. (See article, page 23.)

So the Libya situation is devastating, is precarious, and it's been one of the contributing factors in the massive flood of refugees across the Mediterranean into Europe, which has now become a major crisis for Europe. It's playing out by the hour.

You also have the battlefronts that have been ongoing since 2011 in Syria, which has taken a dramatic turn in recent weeks, to where it's becoming more and more transparently obvious that the government of Turkey is openly supporting the Nusra Front, and de facto supporting the Islamic State, as well. And that the commitment of Turkey, of Saudi Arabia, of Qatar, of Britain, and of the Obama White House is to eliminate the Assad government, even if the result of that is that a Islamic State, or Nusra Front jihadist enclave, is established right on the eastern shores of the Mediterranean.

Now, again, remember that Russian President is aware that all of these destabilizations, all of this activity, is ultimately vectored against Putin, and against Russia. Therefore, there is no option for Russian President Putin to simply sit back at this point, and do nothing, and wait for these events to play out. Russia needs to take a decisive flanking initiative, and at this point, the evidence would strongly suggest that the area where that flanking initiative is about to happen, is in Syria.

kremlin.ru

President Putin's frank discussions with Turkish President Erdogan have not had the necessary deterrent effect. Here, Putin meets Erdogan in Moscow, June 13, 2015.

The Threat in Syria

The situation on the ground in Syria is that the Assad government has been engaged in a four-year war against jihadist rebel forces that have been thoroughly financed and supported from a combination of Turkey, Qatar, Saudi Arabia, in particular, and with Britain always lurking as a kind of divining rod in the background of this whole process.

We're at the point right now where, just in the last several days, since the beginning of this week, there have been news reports coming out of Syria that the Islamic State fighters are now openly using chemical weapons. They've used them in the North of Syria, targetting a village north of Aleppo on at least two occasions. There have been chemical weapons used in Iraq by ISIS forces, battling the Kurdish Peshmerga. And now you have ISIS units that are actually fighting against other rebel forces, but now on the eastern and southern outskirts of the Syrian capital of Damascus.

So, with all of these things going on, inaction is not a viable option from the standpoint particularly of Russian President Putin. The Iranians, as we know, have been involved deeply in providing support ostensibly to the Assad government, and to the military forces under the President Assad regime, but the Iranians have their own ulterior motives. Their concern is

to absolutely secure the position for their allies in Hezbollah, which means that their priority is maintaining control over the mountain areas along the border between Syria and Lebanon. There are certain Alawite and Shi'ite enclaves in the Northern Mediterranean coastal area of Syria, that are also a priority concern for the Iranians.

Russia's Concern

This is very different than the Russian strategic approach. For Russia, the preservation of Syria as a single, unified nation, and with a strong central government in Damascus, is absolutely critical. Russia maintains a major naval port at Tartus, and according to reports in the Syrian newspaper *al-Watan* over the last week, there are plans for Russia to establish a second naval facility in the area nearby Latakia, in the northern coastal area of the country, the reason being that Russia is preparing a potential air intervention into the situation in Syria.

Now some of the early news reporting of this came out of Israel, and there was a certain kind of healthy skepticism about the coverage coming from the Israeli press, for not bad reasons either. But our own *EIR* investigation, our inquiries with some senior intelligence sources here in Washington, indicates that one of the reasons the Israelis are aware of what's going on with the Russians contemplating a major escalation of intervention on behalf of the Assad government, is that Israel maintains air defense along the Syria border.

Israel has been giving overt military assistance to the al-Nusra front, one of the official branches of al-Qaeda in Syria, because, from the Israeli vantage point, Hezbollah poses a greater threat, Under the idea of "my enemy's enemy is my ally," the Israelis have been providing military-medical assistance, and other support to an al-Qaeda apparatus that's been operating and, in effect, controlling the areas around the Israel-Syria border.

This Nusra front would very likely become a priority target for Russian air operations in support of the Syria air force, and therefore, there has to be discussion quietly behind the scenes, between Russian and Israeli government officials, and military officials, to make sure that what is called "de-confliction arrangements" are made; in other words, that when Russia air force operations are taking place in that border area of southern Syria, nearby Israel, Israel will not react, will not activate air defense systems, radar systems, and will not deploy either anti-aircraft or their own fighter jets into the fray.

You see the complexities of this situation, and the dangers of a major escalation into a much larger war, even if it is a regional, and not a general global war. So, the Israelis have reason to be aware of the fact that Russian President Putin is contemplating this kind of action in Syria.

Fronting for ISIS, al-Qaeda

It's also very clear that, despite all of the claims by President Obama and by Turkish President Erdogan, that they are engaged in a "coalition war" against ISIS inside both Iraq and Syria, the reality on the ground is quite different. A year and a half ago, under a thin pretext of being concerned about Syrian Air Force incursions into Turkish airspace, Turkey convened an emergency meeting of NATO, invoked the collective security clause of the NATO charter, and, as a result of that, Patriot missile batteries from Germany, the United States, and other countries, were sent into southern Turkey along the Syrian border.

Dept. of Defense/Glenn Fawcett

NATO Patriot batteries like this one, which sits on an overlook at the Turkish army base of Gaziantep, have kept the Syrian Air Force from suppressing ISIS in northern Syria.

As a result of that, for the last several years, the Syrian Air Force has stayed out of that area, so a significant corridor along the northern part of Syria was off-limits for Syrian Air Force operations against ISIS, and al-Qaeda. In effect, Turkey's actions created a no-fly zone and a safe haven for ISIS and Nusra and other jihadist operations all along the region of northern Syria. President Obama fully has gone along with this. There have been frequent complaints filed by the U.S. Defense Intelligence Agency indicating that the U.S. is misrepresenting the war against the Islamic State, claiming successes when there've been no successes, and, in fact, covering for the fact that de facto, the United States has been backing up ISIS in these operations, particularly in Syria.

Remember that President Obama has never rescinded his commitment to remove Syrian President Bashir Assad from office as a top priority. The Pentagon, the Joint Chiefs of Staff, have a very different view of this, and you may remember that Secretary of Defense Chuck Hagel, in February of this year, was fired by President Obama, or forced to resign, because he was fundamentally opposed to the refusal of the White House to spell out a clear Syria policy.

Now you've got ISIS operating at the gates of Damascus. You have the country facing continuing support for the Islamic State and the Nusra Front coming from the governments of Turkey, Saudi Arabia, Qatar; and now the United States is openly operating with the

Turkish government in a no-fly zone, safe zone operation in the north of Syria. And President Obama, soon after Congress left Washington for the August recess, issued orders to the Pentagon to take direct military action against the Syrian Air Force if there are any actions against the "good" jihadists whom the United States is backing.

Just this past week, Gen. David Petraeus, who is a senior military advisor to the Obama National Security Council, and to the President himself, has been making the argument that the United States should overtly support the activities of the Nusra Front, which, as I say, is the Syrian branch of al-Qaeda, the very people who carried out the 9/11 attacks.

So, President Obama is carrying out a duplicitous policy, and ultimately, the Obama White House is committed to the idea of strategic confrontation with Russia. And so President Putin is seriously considering—no question about it—a flanking military operation by sending Russian Air Force planes and pilots, with teams of logistical support, into Syria, to have them on the ground engaged in directly beefing up the Assad government, and the Assad military forces.

Shifting the Global Geometry

Now, Lyndon LaRouche, in discussions with us this morning and yesterday as well, made the point very clear: This is not a local move by Putin, strictly tied to the situation in Syria. This is a global strategic game-changing, flanking operation by Russia, if Putin goes ahead with it.

And there's every reason to believe, given the nature of the situation, given the profile of Putin himself, given his own experience dealing with the Chechen rebellion and dealing with the Georgian war of several years ago, that he will take this kind of decisive action. He knows, ultimately, that President Obama is a coward and a bully, and that by taking this kind of decisive flanking action in Syria, which is something that is in the vital interests of Russia, and is in the vital interests of anybody looking for stability in

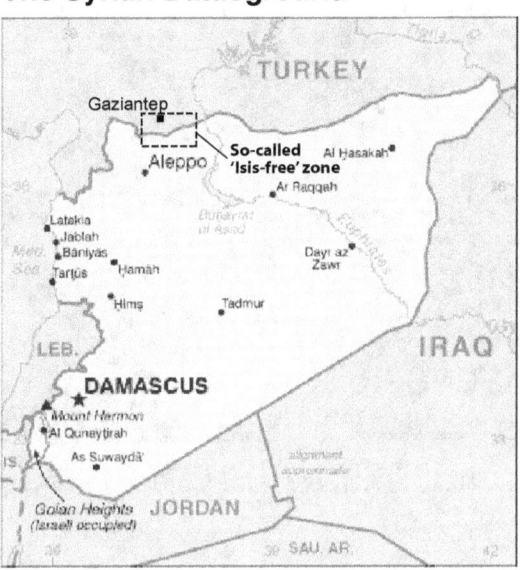

FIGURE 1
The Syrian Battleground

the entire Middle East region, he will put Obama in a real pickle. He also knows that this will deliver a dead-serious message to the Turkish military, and to President Erdogan and others in the AKP party in Turkey, that they'd better back off, because suddenly, there is a prospect of a much bigger and much more volatile war, if they persist in the plan to overthrow Assad, and create a Sunni-jihadist beachhead on the eastern Mediterranean.

So, this is the situation. Now, I think there are a few other elements that are worth bearing in mind as well, as we see how these events unfold over the next few days. As I say, there are credible reports in the Syrian media, in the European press, in the Israeli media, and now more recently, in the U.S.

Plus, discussions that I have personally had with some very senior military and intelligence people here in Washington, indicate that Putin is very likely to act—in a matter of days or hours, perhaps waiting a bit longer to see what kinds of reactions he gets to the threat of this Syria move. But at some point, it is very strongly possible that he will make this move; and this will dramatically alter the global situation.

Remember that among the cadre and fighters of the Islamic State, are an estimated 1,000 Chechens; these are the same Chechen fighters who fought two wars against Russia. And when Putin came in as President of Russia in the late 1990s, he was confronted with an existential crisis in that Chechen situation. He moved absolutely decisively, and crushed the Chechen rebellion. Many of those Chechen fighters fled to Pakistan and Afghanistan, and are now incorporated into both al-Qaeda and into the ISIS offshoot.

So, those seasoned Chechen fighters are part of the potential for destabilization of Russia; and President Putin knows that very well. They also have longstanding established links with the Right-Sector neo-Nazi networks in Ukraine that are pressing for confrontation; a war between Ukraine and Russia, in which NATO would be drawn in to back up Ukraine and the Chechen rebels.

ISIS THREATENS RUSSIA

ISIS's direct threat to Russia was broadcast broadly in this ISIS video, dated September 4, 2014.

How Will Obama React?

This is a strategic play that has many implications and consequences; most emphatically, it will put President Obama into a difficult, if not impossible, situation. Does he persist in supporting the overthrow of Assad, using the Islamic State and the Nusra Front? Does he back down? Does he respond with some kind of new flight-forward provocation?

These are all issues that are on the table; we don't have the answers to them at this point because events are playing out very, very rapidly. And they're playing out in a way that has a built-in element of unpredictability. But it's crucial to understand that the Syria situation now represents a strategic war avoidance opportunity that President Putin of Russia is not likely to overlook or ignore.

Mr. LaRouche emphasized in our discussions both yesterday and today that Putin might have some other things up his sleeve that we're not even thinking about. But for now, it's very clear that the Syria situation represents a preemptive flank; and it's also clear that we've come to a point, between the developments in Ukraine, between the crisis that was created by the Obama overthrow of Qaddafi in Libya, the crisis that has been ongoing for four years in Syria, and in Iraq as well; that all of these things represent a condition of general warfare. We may not yet be at the point where there is large-scale combat on the kind of global scale that we saw in the two world wars of the Twentieth Century, but we are in an environment of warfare.

Under those circumstances, war avoidance can only be accomplished by certain pre-emptive actions; surprise flanking actions that force a resolution of a situation that's otherwise unavoidably on a trajectory toward a much larger general war. In this case, as many U.S., European, and Russian military strategists have been warning in recent weeks, that once such a general war begins, the chances are very, very high that it will turn into a thermonuclear war; perhaps a thermonuclear war of extinction.

So, a great deal is riding on what happens in Syria, and Syria is now a global battlefield. And in the coming days, we will see a certain degree of clarity one way or the other. Even if the Russians were *not* to act there, that itself would have very dramatic strategic consequences. But Mr. LaRouche's view at this point is, barring some other surprise flank, that President Putin is very likely to take some kind of critical action in Syria in the coming days.

II. Britain and the EU

Ogden: Thank you very much, Jeff. Now, our next question is going to be the institutional question for this week; it actually touches on a related aspect of what Jeff just presented. What we'll do is I know Jeff will give some brief remarks to respond to this question in specific; and then Megan Beets will elaborate another aspect which is related to the answer to this question.

So, let me just read the question. It says: "David Cameron has pledged to hold a referendum on continued EU membership of Great Britain by the end of 2017. However, some of his Tory allies are proposing that the referendum be staged as early as April of next year. So the question for Mr. LaRouche is: What are your assessments of the United Kingdom staying or leaving the European Union?"

Jeff, why don't you present Mr. LaRouche's response?

Steinberg: Well, it's kind of like asking whether it makes sense to hang around on the deck of the Titanic for one more drink before jumping into a lifeboat. The situation in the European Union is one of a real process of disintegration. So, on a certain level, for the British to leave the European Union at this point, probably makes a great deal of sense.

The British are survivors; they tend to think in long-wave terms. They've already made it a point by being the first of the European countries to join the Asian Infrastructure Investment Bank; but they have their own recognition that the center of gravity of the world economy has shifted to Asia. They have a lot of stakes on the ground in Europe; and obviously Cameron is trying to negotiate a new set of special relations between Britain and the European Union. What Mr. LaRouche said is, you've got to give a kind of a simple straightforward answer, but at the same time, you've got to be aware that this whole situation is vastly more complex.

We've spoken in recent weeks on this broadcast, about the fact that there's an enormous amount of tumult inside Britain itself. The British monarchy is aging itself not so gracefully out of existence. There is strong resistance to the continuation of the monarchy; there's resistance to the idea of Prince Charles being installed as the next monarch.

You've got the fight inside the British Labour Party; we'll know next week the results of the elections there, where Jeremy Corbyn is expected to win. And he's openly talked about dismantling the structures of the monarchy; starting with bringing an end to the House of Lords. So, there are many unpredictable factors internally in Britain. There are major exposés of the House of Windsor's collusion with the Nazis during the Second World War period; both the installation of Hitler, the war period itself and beyond. So, there are no real simple elements of this.

Now you have two major crises that have put the very existence of the European Union in grave doubt and jeopardy.

Obviously, we've seen fissures within the European Monetary Union and the larger European Union over the handling of the Greek debt crisis; which is really a breakdown crisis of the London-centered trans-Atlantic bank-

creative commons

Jeremy Corbyn, leading candidate for head of the British Labour Party, has challenged the "Royal Perogative," which allows the Monarchy to declare war without parliamentary approval. Here he's seen at a "No More War" event in London.

ing system as a whole. And now, Megan will give us a much more in-depth review of the further dismantling and breakdown into real chaos in Europe as the consequence of President Obama's wars of genocide in North Africa and the Middle East.

So, it makes perfect sense that the referendum date would be significantly moved up, because events are moving at such a rapid pace that to even consider what Europe is going to look like towards the end of 2017, is a kind of exercise in futility. Let me turn things over to Megan for further discussion.

III. Obama's Refugees Besiege Europe

Megan Beets: Thanks, Jeff. So, as Jeff referenced, there is a complete crisis of chaos unfolding in Europe with the influx of hundreds of thousands of refugees fleeing from Obama's wars. Since January of this year, over 350,000 people have flooded the borders of Europe; and I say more than 350,000 because that's just the official detected number of refugees who have arrived at the borders. This number is already 25% higher than all of 2014; this is the biggest refugee and humanitarian crisis since the end of World War II. And this has unleashed utter chaos across an already disintegrating Europe, and has only highlighted the crumbling disunity of the European Union.

As we see manifest in the case of Greece, also in the case of Portugal, Spain, and the complete financial upheaval and collapse, we—not only the people of Europe, or the refugees—we, as mankind, face a complete practical and most importantly a moral, emergency.

The blame for this horror, which I'll outline in a moment for people who haven't closely followed the news reports, is not mysterious; it is placed squarely on the doorstep of President Obama. Where are these refugees coming from? Upwards of 40-50% are fleeing from the wars that Obama began in Syria. Many of them come from Afghanistan, from Eritrea, from Libya, from Sudan, and other places in northern Africa, from Yemen, where the United States' despicable ally Saudi Arabia has been bombing civilian populations. They're coming from Iraq, from the Baltic States, and very significantly, two million people have been displaced from Ukraine. Now, many of those are still in Ukraine, but others are finding ways out; and this is a potential flashpoint for a real emergency and strain on the refugee situation.

Risking Death

To give people a sense of the scale of the floods of human beings coming through the European borders: in July of this year, over the course of one month,

UNHCR/N. Daoud

The flood of Syrian refugees like these, shown crossing into Jordan in February 2012, has grown into a torrent today.

107,500 people officially reached the borders of Europe and entered. Just last week, 23,000 people entered Greece; *23,000 people entered Greece.* That's roughly 3,000 people or more per day, which is 50% more than the previous week.

Now, these people are coming any way that they possibly can. They're coming by boat, in what are unseaworthy vessels crammed with people, many of which sink. They're making very risky border crossings, sometimes in the back of container trucks. They're coming by very dangerous land routes; where they're vulnerable to attack and abuse. And all of this is at great, great risk of death.

Thousands of people are rescued daily. Despite this, over 400 people died in shipwrecks in the Mediterranean in the month of August, bringing the number for this year to 2,600. And people may have seen the very gut-wrenching pictures that are now circulating in the news media of the body of a three-year old Syrian boy, who washed up on the shores when he was drowned attempting to flee from the wars in Syria. Just a couple of weeks ago, the bodies of over 70 people were discovered in the back of a container truck near the border of Hungary and Austria, attempting to cross.

Thousands of people, almost 5,000 people are gathering in Brittany in France, at the opening of the Chunnel, the English Channel Tunnel, preparing to make a

desperate attempt to cross. And several times in the recent weeks the Chunnel had to be shut down because people were discovered in it, attempting to make the crossing to England.

Now, so far this year, around 25,000 people have either died or gone missing in this process; and the numbers are increasing very rapidly.

The people who do successfully make it alive to Europe are entering through countries such as Greece, Italy; they're going from Greece up into Macedonia, they're entering through Hungary. Now, these are the poorest countries in Europe, and current European law dictates that these people must seek asylum in the country which they entered; but these countries can't possibly handle the strain. So, people are running out of food; people who are volunteering to provide food to the refugees are running out of money or capability to provide that food.

There's a complete crisis also in Budapest, Hungary, as thousands of people are currently camped outside and also underground in the train station in Budapest, having purchased train tickets to mostly Germany and other places north into Europe. The Budapest train station was shut down, with dozens upon dozens of armed police barring the doors for these people to enter. These people were in limbo; this morning they did let some of these people board trains; these trains left Budapest and stopped not too far out-side of Budapest, and people were ordered off of the train. Some of these people lay down on the tracks in protest, and got into conflict with the police.

Americans Must Act

I would just urge people, if you haven't, get on the internet; see the pictures, see the news re-ports, see the video coverage, to really put yourself in a position to take in the scale of this crisis. This is a completely untenable situa-tion; the numbers are expected to increase drastically over the second half of 2015. Germany itself expects to take in 800,000 refugees this year.

So far, people in the United States have had very little response or focus on this; as if this is a distant crisis. But, as Jeff iterated, this is not a distant crisis at all. It's absolutely necessary for the people of the United States to dedicate themselves to changing this situation; because the fault absolutely lies with Barack Obama. This is not an abstract crisis; *it was created by the President of the United States.* Every country from which these people flee has been torn apart by an illegal war either started or expanded by President Obama.

Let me just remind people of a few of the impor-tant crisis flashpoints. Back in October 2011, in what was a completely unconstitutional and illegal war, the Obama Administration and NATO forces overthrew the government of Qaddafi, murdering him in Libya under the auspices of a new doctrine of so-called "hu-manitarian intervention," the right to "protect," which was asserted by people within the administration, such as Samantha Powers, who claimed the right to violate the national sovereignty of a nation in the interests of protecting the "humanitarian rights" of the citizens of that country.

This is not a doctrine unique to the Obama Admin-istration; this comes straight from the British. It comes straight from Tony Blair, who is being investigated as a war criminal for the Iraq war, another overthrow of the Westphalian system of national sovereignty. The policy in Libya was a complete continuation of the Bush/

Daily Mail FREE DUVET

DON'T SHOOT!

Battered and bloody, the tyrant of Libya pleads for his life. Moments later, he was dead - executed with a shot to the head

DRAMATIC PICTURES, REPORTS AND ANALYSIS: PAGES 2-11

Blood on Obama's hands: Muammar Qaddafi, killed on October 20, 2011.

Cheney policy in Iraq and Afghani-stan, of war and chaos in the hands of a unitary executive which does not go to Congress to authorize war.

When Qaddafi was overthrown in 2011 in Libya, Mr. LaRouche forecast that this would be the be-ginning of the unleashing of war and chaos across northern Africa and the Middle East.

At roughly the same time, offi-cials from Russia—most emphati-cally then-President Dmitri Medve-dev—also made very clear that it was Russia's view that the policy of undermining of national sover-eignty with so-called "humanitarian interventions" and color revolu-tions, would lead to war; and it would lead to the possible use of nuclear weapons.

Now, Mr. LaRouche's warnings have more than been borne out, as I'm sure people are aware. Jeff out-lined in great detail the kind of crisis and chaos that has spread to Syria with the U.S. and other govern-ments' support of the forces of ISIS and al-Qaeda. This has spread to Yemen, as I referenced in the begin-ning; and it has spread to Ukraine, with the 2013 United States-supported coup of a legitimate govern-ment, and the installation of a Nazi right-wing over-throw which has unleashed the kind of chaos and refu-gee crisis and flashpoint for possible nuclear war.

So, what we're looking at is not some passing event or unexplained condition. This is the kind of crisis you get with the disintegration of civilization. This can only be compared to the situation mankind faced in the Dark Ages with sectarian conflict, with religious war, with increasing rates of death and destruction; and a policy of genocide. People have to ask themselves, "Where is the end of this?"

Oust Obama

There's no practical solution; there's no machina-tion or rearrangement of parts that could possibly end this. Europe is now broken and disintegrating; and it might just be at the hands of the strain of these people who are fleeing into Europe.

The only solution is to oust Obama. The people of the United States must step up and have the courage to declare Obama what he is—a complete criminal who has to be removed from office. These people are coming to Europe because Obama destroyed their homes and terrorized their lives. And he must be put in prison; and that's the point. So, I think that the people of the United States have to face the horror of the situation, and they must act.

Once we decide that, it's very clear what could be done. Emergency measures can and must be taken to meet the immediate needs of the people who are coming to Europe. Programs can and must be started to meet their health needs, the education needs of the children, the training they might need in languages and otherwise to be integrated into the workforce. That must happen, but the only real solution—long-term—has to be found on a higher level; in a completely new paradigm, as we see taking shape with the leadership of China and others in the BRICS nations.

Just very briefly, more specifically on that: In 2012 *EIR* released a white paper special report which was called "A Program for an Economic Miracle in Southern Europe, the Mediterranean Region, and Africa." This report outlined very detailed plans of infrastruc-

ture development corridors which could be created under the kind of credit system which we saw with Franklin Roosevelt in the U.S.; and that we see with the New Development Bank of the BRICS now: to build high speed rail and development corridors which would include transportation, new industrial centers, new canals. We already see an example of this with Egypt's building of the new, expanded Suez Canal. We can integrate nations such as Greece, the regions of the Balkans, the regions of northern Africa, into the new kind of Silk Road initiatives that we see now coming out of China.

So, the programs are there; new power sources, nuclear power. Putting people to work in high-technology jobs; uplifting mankind and giving all people a new possibility for a future. So, the challenge before all of us now, in the context of this very dangerous situation is: Will we have the courage and the morality to act? To throw Obama out; to stop this horror, and to join the rest of humanity.

Ogden: Thank you very much, Megan. In closing, I just want to emphasize that Mr. LaRouche's specific remarks were that "currently, we find ourselves in a situation in which our future is hanging by the thinnest of threads." It's a state of suspense that the world finds itself in, as we look at the opportunity for a flanking action that could be carried out by President Putin, as Jeff elaborated. The increasing rates of death and destruction are being experienced by the peoples of the trans-Atlantic, northern Africa, and southwest Asian regions as every day goes by, emphasize and underscore that a change of the entire world situation—a change which we are on the verge of, a major change— is urgently necessary and must occur, with the necessary leadership coming from those who know how to act.

Before I conclude, I want to draw our viewers' attention to an urgent appeal that was published by Helga Zepp-LaRouche on August 31. It's called "An Urgent Appeal to the United Nations Heads of Government." This is being circulated as a petition in the weeks leading up to the United Nations' General Assembly meeting, which is going to be occurring from Sept. 24 through Oct. 1. [See accompanying article]...

With that said, I want to conclude tonight's broadcast. I'd like to thank Jeff Steinberg and Megan Beets for joining me here in the studio tonight; and I'd like to thank all of you for watching. Please stay tuned to larouchepac.com. Good night.

An Urgent Appeal for Action to Heads of Government: The UN General Assembly Is the World's Last Chance!

by Helga Zepp-LaRouche

Aug. 28—More and more people worldwide are profoundly worried over what only a few prominent people are saying publicly: NATO's confrontation with Russia and China is ongoing, and set to escalate, so that a global thermonuclear war is almost inevitable, unless we dramatically change our political course. The worldwide stock market collapse which followed "Black Monday" wiped out around $5 trillion, which then almost immediately flowed again into the pockets of one gambler or another, after the central banks set their electronic printing presses into motion in grand style.

The ultimate meltdown of the trans-Atlantic financial system has been delayed in the short term by a gigantic dose of "quantitative easing"—the unconditional throwing about of "helicopter money," as former Federal Reserve Chairman Ben Bernanke called it. But it is in this impending financial crash of Wall Street and the

City of London that the source of the acute war danger lies, and not in anything that Russia or China has done.

"Russia is preparing for a conflict with NATO, and NATO is preparing for a possible confrontation with Russia," says a recent study by the "European Leadership Network," which comprises former European and Russian defense ministers and military experts. Indeed, the modernization of tactical nuclear weapons in Europe, the establishment of U.S. BMD systems in Eastern Europe, and NATO's first-strike doctrine permit no other conclusion. Russia and China in turn have reacted with the modernization of their own nuclear capacities and the development of supersonic missiles, which would knock out the NATO systems. If this war were to happen, there is a very high probability that mankind will be largely or totally obliterated.

The heart-wrenching refugee crisis which is cur-

EIRNS/Christopher Lewis

Helga Zepp-LaRouche, at an April 29, 2015 event on the New Silk Road in Frankfurt, Germany.

rently playing out in Europe, and which has resulted from a series of wars based on lies, in Southwest Asia and North Africa, should be a warning shot across the bow for the whole world, that the entire system of the international community of peoples has collapsed. Every single one of the tens of thousands of people who have already drowned in the Mediterranean; every single one of the hundreds of thousands who are currently on the run, only to be potentially exposed to violence by right-wing terrorists; and every single one of the millions who have been uprooted and are now refugees, represents a thundering indictment of those responsible for these war crimes and crimes against humanity.

A New Direction

Where is the institution that can still intervene, virtually at the last minute? Where is the world court before which this great crime can be avenged? Are we, as mankind, collectively able to deflect from a course which is threatening to lead to our own destruction?

If there is any such institution at all, then it is the up-coming General Assembly of the United Nations in New York. A large number of heads of state and government will participate in this meeting from Sept. 24 to Oct. 1. Manhattan, during this time, will be the place where the fate of mankind will be debated before the eyes of the entire world and a vision for a better future can be agreed upon—or, to put it another way: The precondition will be set for whether we will have a future at all.

There is a solution to this existential crisis, but it must be located in a totally new paradigm; it must restore mankind's identity as a creative species, and it must consciously herald a new era for mankind.

Lyndon LaRouche insisted in an emergency appeal issued Aug. 26, that only the immediate introduction of Glass-Steagall banking separation—exactly as Franklin D. Roosevelt introduced it in 1933—can protect the real economy from the effects of the imminent financial meltdown. Wall Street is hopelessly bankrupt. Therefore, an all-out mobilization is required to induce Congress to pre-emptively shut down Wall Street by passing the Glass-Steagall law. Because the crisis is global, the Glass-Steagall standard must be established internationally—i.e., the global financial system must be put through an orderly bankruptcy reorganization and a credit system established, in order to restore the necessary capital-intensive production in the real economy.

The total indebtedness of the global financial system, an estimated $2 quadrillions, of which around 90% is outstanding derivative contracts, is even less

sustainable than Greece's debt. Only if the casino economy is shut down—that is, the virtual and toxic part of the banking sector canceled and the section of the banking system serving the real economy protected—can there be a recovery of the physical economy, thereby halting the dynamic toward war.

The Groundwork Has Been Laid

The UN General Assembly is probably the last opportunity for resolving upon such a reorganization. It is perhaps an historical coincidence that the assembly is occurring in Manhattan, and thus in the place where the first Treasury Secretary of the United States, Alexander Hamilton, established the American System of Economy and the principle of the National Bank. It was precisely in this Hamilitonian tradition that Franklin D. Roosevelt led America out of the Depression in the 1930s, with the Glass-Steagall law and the Reconstruction Finance Corporation. This was also the model by which the Kreditanstalt fuer Wiederaufbau (Reconstruction Loan Corporation) rebuilt Germany out of the rubble after World War II, and made possible the German economic miracle.

Such an economic miracle is needed by many regions of the world today, and its realization is within our grasp. Chinese President Xi Jinping, since 2013, has been putting on the agenda the proposal for building the New Silk Road as a new model for economic cooperation among nations with a perspective of "win-win cooperation."

Since no later than the Summit of the BRICS nations in Fortaleza, Brazil, in 2014, an unprecedented dynamic of cooperation has developed among the BRICS nations, and those of Latin America, Asia, Africa, and even some Europeans, for the realization of long-overdue infrastructure projects: the Nicaragua Canal, a transcontinental railway between Brazil and Peru, several Pacific-to-Atlantic tunnels between Argentina and Chile, extensive cooperation in nuclear energy between the BRICS nations and developing countries, and joint space projects—to name a few. There has been an explosion of development, which had been blocked for decades. The construction of the New Suez Canal in only one year is symptomatic of the new spirit.

What is now demanded of the heads of state at the UN General Assembly, is their capacity to present a vision for mankind. The groundwork has been laid. The construction of the Silk Road Economic Belt and the Maritime Silk Road—"One Belt, One Road"—and its integration with the Eurasian Union is in full swing.

Many states in Asia, Latin America, and Africa are already advancing their development through cooperation with the BRICS countries. All the world's problems could be solved, if this UN General Assembly succeeds in winning the European nations and the United States to cooperate with the BRICS countries, to build up the regions of the world that are currently breaking apart under conditions of war, starvation, water shortages, epidemics, and terrorism.

If this UN General Assembly succeeds, in the framework of the New Silk Road, which is becoming a World Land-Bridge linking peoples together, in adopting a common development perspective, primarily for Southwest Asia and Africa, but also for Central and South America—a perspective for which Russia, China, India, Iran, Egypt, Germany, France, Italy, other European nations, and the United States work together—then it would be relatively simple to overcome terrorism, so that people in these regions have a real perspective for their future, namely to rebuild their states economically. But also, therein lies the only chance for giving the people who are now fleeing from war and terror, hope in their homelands, and for stopping the new migration of many millions of people into an overburdened Europe or America.

Geopolitics, and the idea of solving conflicts through wars, which, in the age of thermonuclear weapons, will lead to the extermination of the human race, must be replaced with the idea of the common aims of mankind, for whose realization all nations on this planet must participate. If the heads of government and other representatives succeed in inspiring their nations with the spirit that they must now, at the moment of the greatest danger for the future survival of mankind, dare to step outside the well-worn pathways of the oligarchical rules of the game, and come to an agreement on the great mega-project for the future of mankind, then we can be confident in the courage to solve all, really *all*, the problems of today, and begin a new era of mankind—an era in which mankind will be truly human and bring our laws and activity here on Earth into harmony with the laws of the order of creation, the Cosmos.

Only in that way will we survive as a species. And by that standard will the heads of state meeting in Manhattan be measured. Because if mankind is going to have a history, it will be remembered either as monsters, or as extraordinary individuals, who succeeded, at the decisive moment, to realize a passionate, tender love for mankind, and usher in a new phase of evolution.

This appeal was translated from German.

On Riemann's Higher Hypothesis of the Flank

by Michael G. Steger

Sept. 6—Russian President Putin's intervention into the crisis now facing the nation of Syria, though laden with risk, may be the preemptive action that ends a thermonuclear world war before it occurs. Whether the American people will respond to this quality of leadership and remove the risk of war, is yet to be seen.

During the attack on Pearl Harbor on December 7, 1941, when facing the threat of global fascism and war, the American people at that time recovered their lost and more compelling identity, and rose to the challenge presented by their great President Franklin Roosevelt. Today, the American people are again asleep in cowardice, with only mild stirrings apparent; yet with over four billion of the world's persons moving to expose the fraud of President Obama and the Wall Street financial system, Americans must soon arise and fulfill that great President's legacy, or face total peril from their own inaction. President Putin, you might say, has turned the flank on the American people as much as he has on Obama and his British controllers' threats of nuclear war.

Consider the moral and existential test of the European migrant crisis, i.e. nothing less than Obama's ongoing Holocaust, and the accelerating destruction of the future of civilization. Then consider the apparent and unequivocal necessity of a new system, one based on the higher principles and implications of the BRICS. Unfortunately, what remains still veiled for many who now recognize the higher moral necessity of a new and global economic system, is that its fulfillment lies infi-

*Bernhard Riemann
(1826-1866)*

nitely far beyond the sphere of mathematics.

Where this necessary future lies, one which prevails not from the past in linear progression, but is provoked as if a surprise from beyond the mathematician's predictable future, and so distinct from the cause of the current collapse, will be found by the method of the great genius Bernhard Riemann and his higher hypothesis of the flank.

Let Riemann then educate those of us who choose to act upon this higher reality, as we now converge upon a moment as great as it is uncertain, a Pearl Harbor-like test of mankind's creative and moral fitness to survive.

The Flank

In a short paper written in 1799, a young Carl F. Gauss, Riemann's later mentor, launched what was to be a lifelong attack against the fraud of what was to become Napoleon Bonaparte's fascist regime, a regime no less dependent on the tyranny of mathematics than today's trans-Atlantic rot.

Gauss was thus quickly identified by Napoleon's leading agents, e.g. Joseph-Louis Lagrange and Pierre-Simon Laplace, as the successor to the great European tradition in physical science, one premised upon the powers of creative genius towards the discovery of principle. In particular, as was obvious to Napoleon's henchmen, what Gauss had presented in 1799 was an irrefutable defense of the great genius Gottfried Leibniz, whose death in 1716 had opened the gates to a British-directed cult of mathematics, but who, while living, not only dominated the intellectual culture of Europe during the previous century, but had also led a major political intervention into the growing dominance of the Anglo-Dutch financial empire.

Now, under the tyranny of Napoleon, and the later impositions of the fascist Congress of Vienna, Gauss was forced to operate behind a veil of seemingly mathematical advancements, or face certain destruction for his devotion to the creative potential of the human mind. [1]

Yet, each area of Gauss' development of the language of mathematics was premised entirely upon the most rigorous and extensive physical investigations, each resolved by a quality of physical insight entirely coherent with, and often in direct continuation of the work of Nicholas of Cusa, Johannes Kepler, and Gottfried Leibniz before him. [2]

---

1. Gauss's so-called mathematical work was so prolific and penetrating that he is considered to this day the most dominant figure in the creation of modern mathematical studies.
2. For example, Gauss's investigation of curvature was premised on what was then the most extensive geodetic survey ever attempted, a process similar and very much conceptually related to the discovery by Johannes Kepler of physical gravitation as presented in his *Nova Astro-*

For Gauss. the mathematics was in every case an after-effect, a remnant of a physical discovery. But by the time of Napoleon's defeat and the Congress of Vienna's enforcement of the *ancien régime* and brutal dictatorship over Europe, the tyranny of mathematics was only strengthened against Gauss' scientific leadership.

So Gauss, left to his own devices, rejected the mathematicians' world view and continued his own remarkable advancements in scientific thought over the next half-century. Much like Albert Einstein, who was later to express his own theological objections while facing similar political affronts, i.e. "God doesn't play dice," Gauss remained constrained under persistent political attacks, relegating his creative revenge to a later date.

Turning the Flank

By 1854 Bernhard Riemann had become one of Gauss' leading students and a leading scientific thinker at the renowned Goettingen University. He was one of the few young scientists who would survive the mathe-

---

nomia. To this day, Gauss' work in this area lays the basis for understanding partial differential equations, field theory, and relativity; yet his physical investigations, let alone his remarkable insights such as his discovery of the asteroid Ceres, are largely ignored or overlooked.

Mathematical Demons

Pierre-Simon Laplace, a henchman for mathematics and a leading Bonapartist, known best for his attack against physical astronomy, i.e. the very system of discovery of principle developed by Cusa and Kepler, published his diatribe in support of British empiricism and mathematical astronomy entitled *Mécanique Céleste* in that very same year of 1799.

Laplace, who was infamous for denying the existence of God based on his mathematical assumptions, later expressed his world view in 1814 as a companion to his study of probability, where he describes what is now known as Laplace's demon:

> We may regard the present state of the universe as the effect of its past and the cause of its future. An intellect which at a certain moment would know all forces that set nature in motion, and all positions of all items of which nature is composed, if this intellect

were also vast enough to submit these data to analysis, it would embrace in a single formula the movements of the greatest bodies of the universe and those of the tiniest atom; for such an intellect nothing would be uncertain and the future just like the past would be present before its eyes.

> —Pierre-Simon Laplace,
> *A Philosophical Essay on Probabilities* (1814)

That is to say, there is no future except that which has already been decided by past events. No fundamental advancements, no revolutions in scientific thought, nor transformations of the global economy would or could occur unless they have already been predetermined by the total set of previous interactions, a property later ascribed also to the fraudulent second law of thermodynamics.

In other words, one must accept Laplace's stupidity and our early death, for creativity and God have been reduced to what one might call an incestuous mechanics.

maticians' attacks, though not for long—but unlike others less fortunate, such as Niels Abel and Evariste Galois, who would perish early, due to brutal attacks by Laplace's lackeys Cauchy and Poisson.

With his aging mentor, the leading European genius, sitting in the audience, Riemann presented his Habilitation Dissertation, which launched,—much as his mentor had in 1799 but now with even greater powers of insight as a result of Gauss' half-century of work—what would redefine the entire nature of physical science in accordance with the principles of physical discovery of universal principle, freeing mankind from the tyranny of mathematics.

Riemann's mentor, Carl Friedrich Gauss (1777-1855), painted by Christian Albrecht Jenson.

Riemann, through his brilliant philosophical investigation, had captured, by way of a conceptual development of Gauss's unique contributions, the essence of mathematical thought as applied to physical principle, only to then expose its intrinsic failure to provide any benefit to future scientific discovery. It was a conclusion which triggered many resentments, but a great joy to Gauss, and then Einstein later, and to all who love mankind's unique creative potential as against our current depravity.

For Riemann, in taking up the underlying problem of mathematics over the preceding 2,000 years, beginning with the formal system of Euclid, had set his sights not on a revolution in the scientific world view, which had then become so depraved as to worship Isaac Newton even in Germany, but rather set himself the goal of a revolution in the foundations of scientific thought itself. [3]

His foundations for this most remarkable flanking

maneuver—an intervention which has in essence defined the character of the domain by which a revolution in human thought occurs, i.e. the domain from which all successful advancement in human culture depends, including Putin's now critical action in Syria—were Gauss' unique advancements regarding the nature of universal gravitation, combined with the psychological insights of a student of the poet Friedrich Schiller, Johann Herbart, and his work regarding the topological characteristics of the development of the creative mind itself. [4] [5]

Unknown to most then or now, once Riemann premised his investigation upon Gauss's most advanced investigations into the nature of physical space, his was no longer an investigation of space itself, but rather that which determines the characteristics of space, i.e. the physical principles which determine the metrics and actions within physical space, an idea entirely outside the confines of eunuchs such as Euclid, and one which brought sheer delight to Einstein's reflections on the pathway of light a half century later! [6]

---

3. From Riemann's *Habilitation Dissertation*: "*Plan of the Investigation.* It is known that geometry assumes, both the notion of space and the first principles of constructions in space, as given in advance. She gives definitions of them which are merely nominal, while the true determinations appear in the form of axioms. The relation of these assumptions remains consequently in darkness; we perceive neither whether and how far their connection is necessary, nor *a priori*, whether it is possible. From Euclid to Legendre (to name the most famous of modern reforming geometers) this darkness was cleared up neither by mathematicians nor by such philosophers as concerned themselves with it." Clifford Version.

4. This should come as no surprise to any student of Kepler's *Harmony of the World,* where Kepler's own rigorous pursuit of the principle of gravitation led him deeper and deeper into reflections on the nature of creative mind as a principle itself.

5. From the *Habilitation Dissertation*: "In proceeding to attempt the solution of the first of these problems, the development of the notion of a multiply extended magnitude, I think I may the more claim indulgent criticism in that I am not practised in such undertakings of a philosophical nature where the difficulty lies more in the concepts themselves than in the construction; and that besides some very short hints on the matter given by Privy Councillor Gauss in his second memoir on Biquadratic Residues, in the *Göttingen Gelehrte Anzeige*, and in his Jubilee-book, and some philosophical researches of Herbart, I could make use of no previous labours."

6. From the *Habilitation Dissertation*: "The question of the validity of the hypotheses of geometry in the infinitely small is bound up with the question of the basis of the metric relations of space. In this last question, which we may still regard as belonging to the doctrine of space, is found the application of the remark made above; that in a discrete manifold, the basis of its metric relations is given in the notion of it, while in a continuous manifold, this basis must come from outside. Either therefore the reality which underlies space must form a discrete manifold, or we must seek the basis of its metric relations outside it, in binding forces which act upon it."

Two views of a geometric model of hydrodynamic shock-wave generation, which Riemann studied, and led to one of his revolutionary contributions to scientific thought.

As Riemann posits this in the final assertion and conclusion of his dissertation, with future discovery lingering just beyond, he resolves the greatest of flanks:

"This leads us into the domain of another science, that of physics, into which the object of today's proceedings [in the math department] does not allow us to enter."

It is from this vantage point that Riemann makes his critical turn, the final *fait accompli*. For once the positive identification of physical principles is sufficiently made, an assertion which can only conjure images of a proud and smiling Gauss—an assertion such as the "binding forces which act upon it (i.e. space),"—then, in this context, all of the previous mathematical assumptions and infinite language constructions which had become the subject of extensive academic study, all at once become obsolete, the mere remnants of past discoveries at best.

So even while Gauss' investigations, especially into the questions of curvature, had provided a most rigorous identification of the physical characteristics of Kepler's principle of gravitation, yet the mathematical concepts are unable by their own limitations, to ever provide a reproduction of Kepler's discovery. Gauss would be the first to acknowledge such a point, but it was a point left for his student Riemann to make.

For the re-creation of Kepler's discovery of harmonic orderings of gravitation, or of Einstein's development of general relativity, or perhaps most important, the coming discovery of the principle of our galaxy according to higher relativistic harmonic orderings, are not dependent upon mathematical conceptions,—indeed, usually greatly hindered by them,—but depend rather on the physical insights and musical passion of the likes of Kepler, Gauss, Riemann and Einstein, as well as Bach, Mozart, and Beethoven. For such discoveries will not be found in the domain of mathematics or contemplations of space, but rather in the increasing potential of the human individual to apply the great discoveries of the past as an impassioned foundation and source of optimism to access the necessary and sufficient future, projected uniquely onto the creative mind of man.

Epilogue

Since the subject of our proceedings does permit an investigation into the domain of physics, it is entirely appropriate to provide an important, if perhaps introductory, consideration towards an immediate change in the global systemic nature of the human economy.

Take as an example the five Platonic solids. Why five? Could you have foreseen that only five regular polyhedra exist in physical space? Such considerations uniquely provide an opportunity to reflect on the assumptions which shape our conception of human history.

It is not unusual when confronting the typical pessimist, perhaps even a devotee of Donald Trump, that they profess such despair simply because they have already accepted defeat, i.e. their assumptions of the shape of human history do not permit revolutionary development. Unbeknownst to the average pessimist, they have accepted assumptions about the nature of human history, for which, as Riemann states at the beginning of his dissertation, "The relation of these assumptions remains consequently in darkness; we perceive neither whether and how far their connection is necessary, nor *a priori*, whether it is possible."

To the revolutionary political activist, as contrasted to the common spectator or political pundit, it is increasingly obvious that we are now converging on a discontinuous moment in the course of human history, one which stems not from past events, but from the future's necessity, either significantly downwards with great loss of human life and culture, and even possible extinction,—or upwards to a new, greater existence for mankind as a creative species. Such singular moments are what human history is made of: not from the past, but from our Galaxy's to-be-discovered future.

Obama Is to Blame for the Refugee Catastrophe; We Urgently Need a Coalition Against ISIS!

by Helga Zepp-LaRouche

Sept. 4—The worst refugee disaster since the end of World War II, in which millions of people are on the run from war, bestial terror gangs, hunger, and disease, is not the result of regional processes in the Middle East or Africa, but rather of a deliberate policy by Barack Obama, David Cameron, NATO, and the European Union (EU). If this obvious fact does not lead to a change in policy, the flow of desperate people trying to escape death by going to Europe will swell to many more millions. According to the United Nations High Commissioner on Refugees (UNHCR), there were already 60 million people, worldwide, in flight by the end of 2014, before the recent explosion.

The *Washington Post* announced self-righteously on September 4, under the headline "Europe's abdication," the moral and legal abdication of "European Christian culture," since it is meeting the refugees with "indifference, contempt, or the cold hostility of barbed wire and racism." What the paper covers up, with typical media-spin, is the fact that it was President Obama,—and Bush and Cheney before him,—who caused the devastation of the greater part of the Middle East and North Africa, and thus the resulting refugee catastrophe, through a whole series of wars which were built on lies; and through the two administrations' deliberate and intentional support for al-Qaeda, al-Nusra, and ISIS, in order to overthrow the elected governments of Iraq, Libya, and Syria, one after the other.

Gen. Flynn Spills the Beans

In an unprecedented interview with the television network Al-Jazeera on July 31st of this year, General Michael Flynn, the former head of the U.S. Defense Intelligence Agency, accused the Obama Administration of intentionally—and not as a result of miscalculation—backing the ISIS organization, knowing full well that the intention of ISIS was to build an "Islamic caliphate" on the territory of Iraq and Syria. Even earlier, in May, a memorandum of the DIA from 2012 was made public due to a lawsuit by the organization Judicial Watch. It contained an analysis which found that the U.S. supply of weapons from Qaddafi's arsenal to the Syrian rebels would encourage their intention to establish an Islamic caliphate. Lt. General Flynn stressed that the policy of the White House was not an oversight, but a deliberate intention.

NATO

UK Prime Minister Tony Blair and President George W. Bush, perpetrators of the 2003 war on Iraq, at a NATO meeting in Turkey in June 2004.

Gen. Flynn had been forced to resign from the post of DIA chief, after the reports produced under his authority had prompted the U.S. Chief of Staff Martin Dempsey to call off the planned U.S. military strike against Syria in September 2013 at the last moment, in a successful intervention against Obama.

In November 2012, Turkey had officially asked NATO for help, supposedly for protection against the Syrian Air Force which posed no serious threat to Turkey at that time. In response, the foreign ministers of the 28 NATO states approved the deployment of Patriot missiles, with the participation of Holland and Germany. Earlier, then-U.S. Secretary of Defense Leon Panetta had already ordered the relocation of two Patriot units to Turkey. The Defense Secretary stressed explicitly that the missiles were expected to be used exclusively for the defense of Turkey, *not* to establish a no-fly zone over Syria.

But this was precisely the intention behind Erdogan's action. Erdogan, like the U.S. government, wanted to eliminate Assad, and to this end had supported various rebel groups in Syria, while attacking the only effective fighting force against ISIS by bombing the Kurds.

The mere presence of the Patriot missile defense systems in the Turkish province of Hatay was a major factor that enabled the al-Nusra organization, which is associated with al-Qaeda, to gain control of the province of Idlib and parts of Aleppo province, north of the city of Aleppo in Syria. In fact, the radar systems of Patriot missiles ranged far beyond the Turkish-Syrian border and prevented the Syrian Air Force from fighting the advancing jihadists. This obviously corresponded to Erdogan's intention,—when he requested the NATO air defense,—to establish a no-fly zone in Syria, under which the IS could operate with impunity. How could the military have overlooked that?

Russians Corroborate the Charge

The same view as that of General Flynn,—that the Obama Administration had deliberately built up ISIS, and therefore is responsible for the refugee catastro-

White House/Pete Souza
Barack Obama and his top U.S. and NATO commander in Afghanistan, Gen. David Petraeus—facilitators of the rise of ISIS—in November 2010.

phe,—has now also been expressed by the head of the Russian Republic of Chechnya, Ramzan Kadyrov. His father, the former president of Chechnya Akhmad Kadyrov, fell victim on May 9, 2004 to a bombing for which the Chechen Islamist rebel leader Shamil Basayev had claimed responsibility. Earlier, the American National Endowment for Democracy (NED), a source of funding for "color revolutions" around the globe, had provided handsome contributions to radical Islamists, who, during the two Chechen wars in the '90s, had already tried to establish an Islamic caliphate!

Ramzan Kadyrov recently told the press that he was in possession of information indicating that the former CIA chief and commander of the coalition forces in Iraq and Afghanistan, General David Petraeus, had personally recruited the leader of ISIS, Abu Bakr al-Baghdadi, to work on behlaf of the United States. As the *Süddeutsche Zeitung* reported on September 2, the same Petraeus is now proposing to woo away members of the al-Nusra Front—the al-Qaeda offshoot—and use them against the IS. The current head of IS, Abu Bakr al-Baghdadi, who, according to Kadyrov, is an asset of Petraeus, had previously been the founder of al-Nusra.

This madcap suggestion by Petraeus clearly launches another chapter in the unending saga of the American policy that began as early as 1975 with Zbigniew Brzezinski's plan to play the so-called "Islamic card"—at that time against the Soviet Union—and to train Afghan Mujahideen to fight the Soviets. That's where these insane policies began, and since then, the United States,—and of course, the British,—have trained a continual series of "good rebels," which are then deployed for regime change against sovereign states. The "good rebels" then become terrorists who turn against their trainers; the trainers then launch military strikes and drone attacks against them, which in turn produce more terrorists, against whom one must then recruit new "good rebels" who again turn against their trainers as terrorists, etc., etc.

National Endowment for Democracy President Carl Gershman, and his Senior Director for Europe and Eurasia, Nadia Diuk—out to overthrow governments worldwide.

This chain of events has continued now for 40 years and has not only transformed Iraq, Afghanistan, Syria, Yemen, Libya, and much of sub-Saharan Africa into a hell; the ultimate goal is regime change in Russia and China. And that's a policy that would lead, with absolute certainty, to the third and final world war.

Go the Root

It will not be sufficient to treat the symptoms of this crisis. Of course, it is important to take action against the gangs smuggling illegal immigrants. But as of now the police and judiciary, as *Der Spiegel* headlined, are "absolutely stretched to their limits." Again, one must go at the roots of the problem.

For example: The smugglers in Libya, who send desperate people from Africa to their deaths in ridiculous boats on the Mediterranean Sea, are the same people whom Obama brought to power in his campaign against Qaddafi. The war correspondent for the Italian newspaper *Il Giornale*, Gian Micalessin, reported in the April 20 issue that the Obama Administration-backed government of the "Fajr Libya" ("Libyan Dawn") in Tripoli controls the smuggling of human beings across the Mediterranean. "Fajr Libya" is dominated by the Muslim Brotherhood and the Libyan Islamic Fighting Group (LIFG), which was used by Obama and the Saudi Wahhabis to brutally eliminate Qaddafi. Today this grouping has a firm grip on human trafficking from Sudan, Chad, and Niger, and pockets between 800 and 1500 euros per refugee.

Of course, it is absolutely necessary to ensure that these refugees receive the aid to which they are entitled under the Geneva Convention. We have to really integrate them into the work force and society. But much more is needed. The hideous spectacle that the EU has provided in this crisis, inter alia, with their ongoing sanctions against Syria—and thus against the Syrian civilian population—demonstrates that an alliance that exists only on the basis of a monetary union and the interests of the banks, and is otherwise only the regional branch the Anglo-American empire, is worth absolutely nothing if real challenges emerge. We must draw the conclusion that we need a different Europe—one that has a vision and a solution for the problems that are now manifesting themselves in the refugee crisis.

The Sept. 3 military parade in Beijing demonstrated in a unique way that the strategic cards have been reshuffled. China and Russia have forged a close alliance, and the strategic superiority of the United States has been called into question by the Dongfeng-21D ("East Wind") missile, which was presented at the parade as a means for combatting aircraft carriers. These missiles, flying at ten times the speed of sound, cost only one twelve hundredth of the cost of the American aircraft carrier which they can neutralize.

It's time for Germany and the other nations in Europe to adjust to the prospect of a win-win cooperation between sovereign states on this planet, and cease to be the mindless lap-dogs of governments in Washington, which don't care about the interests of the American people, or even, in the slightest, the interests of Europeans. If we want to solve the refugee catastrophe, we have to seize this crisis as an opportunity to give Germany and Europe a completely new orientation.

UN Documents War Crimes of Obama's Operatives

by William F. Wertz, Jr.

Sept. 5—More than six months ago, on Feb. 23, 2015, the "UN Security Council Panel of Experts on Libya" issued a detailed report on the chaos that has been spreading from that country since the 2011 overthrow and execution of Muammar Qaddafi. More and more of northern Africa and the eastern Mediterranean are being made into Twenty-First Century replicas of Dark Age hellholes. Refugees by the thousands are trying to flee to Europe. The world knows all this, but who is doing anything but ignoring it and the responsibility for these crimes against humanity?

Weapons Trafficking

Obama launched the war to overthrow Qaddafi in Libya, throwing his support to the al-Qaeda affiliated Libyan Islamic Fighting Group (LIFG). Weapons were provided to the LIFG by Obama through Qatar and the UAE. Once Qaddafi had been assassinated, this same al-Qaeda-affiliated LIFG network then ran weapons seized from Libyan stockpiles to al-Qaeda and ISIS terrorist organizations in Syria and throughout Africa. (See "Updated Fact Sheet: Obama's Saudi Connection; the Obama—al-Qaeda Alliance" The UN Report findings are damning.)

Numbers indicate sections of the report on Libya by the UN Panel of Experts.

200. The Panel visited Chad, Egypt, Niger, Tunisia, and the Syrian Arab Republic, countries that have been affected by the proliferation of weapons since the beginning of the Libyan uprising.

201. Information gathered indicates that arms originating from Libya have significantly reinforced the military capacity of terrorist groups operating in different parts of the region, including in Algeria, Egypt, Mali, and Tunisia in particular.

202. The Tunisian authorities told the Panel that most military matériel used in terrorist activities came from Libya.

203. Egypt continues to be among the primary destinations for Libyan weapons. Transfers to Gaza through Egypt are also continuing. While the Syrian Arab Republic was a significant destination for Libyan arms during the first two years of the conflict, that trend appears to have faded in the past 12 to 24 months.

204. Several arms-trafficking networks have established themselves in the south of Libya since the revolution, continuing to draw on stockpiles diverted during and after the revolution. This guarantees sustained proliferation outside the country, particularly towards southern Algeria, Niger, Chad, and Sudan.

205. With the absence of State control over the south of Libya since the revolution, and the development of regional terrorist groups, concerns have been growing about the southern region becoming a strategic zone for terrorist groups in the Sahel, especially in terms of training, funding, rest and recuperation, recruitment and acquisition of military matériel. Matériel coming from Libya and destined for terrorist groups in Mali was seized or destroyed on several occasions in 2014 in Niger by the French-led Operation Barkhane.

Human Trafficking

The same UN Security Report also reports on the involvement of the terrorist groups in Libya in running the lucrative migrant business.

195. The Panel interviewed several professionals working on the issue of illegal migration to Europe via the Mediterranean Sea. They stated that the transnational networks organizing the human trafficking had agents embedded within the Libyan armed groups controlling territory along the smuggling routes. The armed groups provide access and help secure those operations in exchange for a fee. Most of the illegal immigrants are picked up from unseaworthy vessels by the Italian navy and coast guard. The role of Libya in the illegal immigration is pivotal. Italian officials explained to the Panel that, of 167,184 immigrants rescued at sea in 2014, 141,484, or 85%, had left from the Libyan coast.

196. The human trafficking business generates considerable income. The migrants, mainly from West Africa and the Horn of Africa, have to pay traffickers for the stages of their voyage. Migrants debriefed in Italy explained that the prices for the last leg alone, the boat crossing, ranged between $800 and $2,000, depending on sea conditions, vessel type, port of departure, and travel class. This means that, for an average price of $1,200 per migrant, the last part of the smug-

gling chain generated a total turnover of almost $170 million in 2014. Most illegal migrants leave from the western coastline of Libya. The Panel has not been able to confirm the names of militias and militia leaders involved, but continues to investigate the matter.

197. Armed groups control several important border crossings and entry points, allowing them to take percentages on ongoing trade and smuggling operations, including of drugs, arms, commodities and fuel.

Torture

Recently, it has been revealed that Muammar Qaddafi's third son, Saadi Qaddafi, who is held in Hadba prison, which is under the control of LIFG's Khalid al-Sharif, has been subjected to torture. A video was released by Arabic Clear News which shows Saadi Qaddafi being whipped on the soles of his feet by three unidentified individuals. Qaddafi's lawyer has called the treatment "an international crime, crime of torture and cruel and inhumane treatment."

Human Rights Watch

Obama ally Khalid al-Sharif, once deputy emir of the Libyan Islamic Fighting Group, now runs the Libyan National Guard.

The same UN Security Council Report indicates that it is fully aware of such torture perpetrated by Khalid al-Sharif's National Guard which runs the prison.

79. First, the Panel has received consistent reports of serious human rights abuses at Hadba prison in Tripoli. The prison is controlled by militiamen supervised by Khaled al-Sharif and are commonly referred to as the National Guard, which was the armed group commanded by al-Sharif during the revolution.

Some of the Key War Criminal Underlings

Although the UN report states that it has been unable to confirm the names of the militias and militia leaders involved, the same report does indeed identify the role of key leaders of the LIFG, who were backed by Obama to overthrow Qaddafi, and then used in the effort to overthrow President Assad of Syria.

One of the key persons identified in the report is Khalid al-Sharif. Khalid al-Sharif was appointed on Jan. 11, 2013, to be the deputy minister of defense of

Libya. He was previously the deputy emir of the al-Qaeda-linked LIFG, and as such, he was the LIFG military commander.

After the takeover of Tripoli, he worked with the Tripoli Military Council headed by Abdel Hakim Belhadj, who is the emir of the LIFG. Khalid al-Sharif then went on to form the National Guard, which works directly with the Border Guard and the Judicial Police in supervising many prisons. Although Khalid al-Sharif has since been sacked as the deputy minister of defense, he continues to run the National Guard, which has over 10,000 fighters at its disposal.

In sections 134, 135, and 143 of their Report, the Panel of Experts states that in his position as deputy minister of defense of Libya, Khalid al-Sharif bypassed the official Military Procurement Department of the Libyan Defense Ministry to sign authorizations for and to distribute weapons to terrorist groups.

142. In November 2014, the Panel inspected the cargo of the vessel Nour M, seized in Greece in November 2013, and including 55 containers and more than 32 million rounds of ammunition (1,103 tons) for assault rifles and machine guns, on their way to Tripoli. The Greek authorities provided the Committee and the Panel with full information and documentation. The latter indicated that the shipper was Ukrinmash, a Ukrainian State company, the consignee was the Ministry of Defence of Libya, and that the deal was brokered by TSS Silah Ve Savunma Sanayi Dis Ticaret Limited Sirkett, a Turkish company. The vessel belonged to TSS Group Tutun Sigara Sanayi Ve, another Turkish company. To date, Greece has not commenced any prosecution relating to this case of violation.

143. The note from the Libyan authorities confirming to the Ukrainian authorities that the Libyan authorities were ready to accept the cargo was signed by Khaled al-Sharif.

Wissam bin Hamid

On the night of Sept. 11, 2012, Wissam bin Hamid was the go-to man for Obama when the U.S. mission and CIA annex came under attack. Wissam bin Hamid is head of Libya Shield I. It was he who met the U.S. soldiers at the Benghazi Airport that fateful night. First he delayed the U.S. relief forces for approximately three hours from departing the airport to go to the CIA annex. Then his forces accompanied the U.S. forces to the CIA annex, which shortly thereafter came under mortar attack. After the attack, he helped to escort the

Obama ally Wissam bin Hamid, commander of Libya Shield at the time of the Benghazi attack, and today, working with Ansar al-Sharia in Benghazi on behalf of the Islamic State.

bodies of the four Americans killed that night in Benghazi to the airport.

When the FBI finally went to Benghazi to investigate the attacks, it was Wissam bin Hamid who was relied upon to escort them and provide them with protection.

In August 2012, just before the Sept. 11 Benghazi attack, the U.S. Library of Congress issued a report entitled *Al-Qaeda in Libya: A Profile*. In that report it was stated that Wissam bin Hamid was the head of al-Qaeda in Libya. The report also reported that Mokhtar bel Mokhtar, the head of al-Qaeda in the Maghreb, had been his special invited guest at a demonstration in March 2012 in the city of Sirte.

When Wissam bin Hamid met with a U.S. advance team in Benghazi days before the arrival of Ambassador Chris Stevens, he reported to a U.S. official that if his favored Muslim Brotherhood candidate for Libya Prime Minister did not win an upcoming election, the Libya Shield would not continue to guarantee security in Benghazi.

Where is Wissam bin Hamid today? According to the Panel's report, Wissam bin Hamid is working with Ansar al-Sharia in Benghazi on behalf of the Islamic State.

44. Benghazi Revolutionaries Shura Council figureheads Mohammed al-Zahawi (Ansar al-Sharia), Wissam bin Hamid (Libya Shield I), and Jalal Makhzoum (Rafallah al-Sahati brigade) have been featured together in several pictures and videos that were made during or after military operations, showing that the alliance also exists at an operational level. Their recorded speeches and written statements confirm that the coalition has little interest in the stabilization of the Libyan state. The Benghazi Revolutionaries Shura Council has made repeated statements rejecting Libyan democracy and stressing the need to install the rule of God. As such, and this is confirmed by their actions, these groups appear more interested in establishing strict sharia rule than in politics in Tripoli.

Ansar al-Sharia leader Mohammed al-Zahawi was reported to have announced the establishment of an Islamic emirate on Radio Tawahid (Islamic Unification).

48. The commander of the eastern Libya Shield brigade, Wissam bin Hamid, had previously been accused by Coptic Christians of running a detention facility where they underwent torture. Sources, including a victim, confirmed to the Panel that bin Hamid was frequently involved in arbitrary arrests, sometimes to obtain ransoms and benefit financially.

49. Furthermore, the Panel has seen several pictures on social media, allegedly showing the Islamic Youth Shura Council organizing rallies in support of Islamic State.

The UN report merely confirms that Wissam bin Hamid today is precisely what the U.S. Library of Congress report said he was prior to Benghazi. And this is the man Obama relied upon to provide security for our forces in Benghazi! It is hardly credible that the U.S. Library of Congress would have better intelligence than the intelligence available to the President. One can only come to the conclusion, reached by Gen. Michael Flynn, that the policy pursued by Obama was a "willful decision."

Abdul Hakim Belhadj

Belhadj was the emir of the al-Qaeda-affiliated Libyan Islamic Fighting Group before, with Obama's support, he became the head of the Tripoli Military Council after Qaddafi was forced to flee the city. Approximately one week after being named commander of the Tripoli Military Council, in August 2011, Belhadj travelled to Qatar where he met with NATO officials. Did the NATO officials not know that Belhadj was al-Qaeda?

youtube

Obama ally Abdel Hakim Belhadj, formerly head of the Libyan Islamic Fighting Group, and now reportedly a commander for ISIS in Libya.

Where is Belhadj today? According to Global Research, "Belhadj has now firmly ensconced himself as the organizational commander of the ISIS presence inside Libya. The information comes from an unnamed U.S. intelligence official who has confirmed that Belhadj is supporting and coordinating the efforts of the ISIS training centers in eastern Libya around the city of Derna, an area long known as a hotbed of jihadi militancy."

'The Life of Humanity Depends Upon the Ability To Recognize This Different Voice That We're About To Hear, Now'

This is a transcript of excerpts from Lyndon LaRouche's Dialogue *with the Manhattan Project on Saturday, September 5, 2015.*

Dennis Speed: My name is Dennis Speed, and on behalf of the LaRouche Political Action Committee, I want to welcome everybody here today. We're in a situation which is literally momentarily evolving as we speak. We're going to go right into it. I simply want to refer to a statement that Helga LaRouche issued: She had one particular section I just want to refer to. She said, "Manhattan, during this time, will be the place where the fate of mankind will be debated before the eyes of the entire world and a vision for a better future can be agreed upon."

That's what we're doing here. That's what we're doing here today, and that's what we're doing on the eve of the convening of the heads of state at the United Nations. But, it's the institution of the American Presidency, of the Hamiltonian Presidency, that is the only institution that can save mankind, and it's that, to which, as you know, Mr. Lyndon LaRouche has called our attention.

Lyn, I'm going to ask you first if you have some things you'd like to say to us all, and then we'll go

EIRNS/Suzanne Klebe

Diane Sare, who currently runs the Manhattan Community Chorus, here conducts a Schiller Institute chorus in Bach's Magnificat in Trenton, New Jersey in June of 2013.

We've now come to the point where the relations among nations have to be changed, that nations must come to a moral standard of productivity, of creativity, of rising to higher achievements; of exploring space, developing the galaxy, which is an essential task before us in the times to come. So, it's a new period. And therefore the important thing is to mobilize the population of the United States, of Germany, of Russia, of China, and China and Russia are very much on this case right now.

right to questions from there.

Lyndon LaRouche: Obviously there is a fundamental change in the manner of society today. It's coming out that Putin has made a move; it's a very key move. It coincides with what happened with China during the last week, and that was a coincidence there. But now everything is changing.

Everything is going into a great change, throughout Europe and throughout the United States. And we have to, as a nation, pull this together, because the life of humanity at large depends upon the ability to recognize this different voice, which we are about to hear, now.

Speed: Okay, very good. So, let's go right to questions.

Q: Good afternoon, Lyn. This is B— from New Jersey. Given what seems to be at first glance a totally chaotic situation in the Middle East,—but clearly there are a lot of complexities, particularly around the Syria and other situations, which have to be addressed— Putin and others are trying to navigate those complexities to come out with an effect which they know has to be taken at this point. So could you go through some of that?

LaRouche: Yes. Well, what's happened essentially, is that this has been going on for a long period of time, and finally it's come to a point of a crucial point where things have to change. And what's typical right now, which I think before we probably get back into this discussion a little later, because we don't want to clutter everything up and make it confusing.

But a few points: What's happened is that the meeting of Putin with China on the case of the Chinese occasion [Sept 3 VJ Day celebration], has been echoed again by Putin. And the idea is to move the world out of Obama, and out of the British system, which are two very similar kinds of things.

Other things involve questions which can be answered. The problem is that the questions which should be answered cannot be answered by certain governments, including the United States government right now.

For example, what's the situation? The United States government is *totally bankrupt*. Now, how is the U.S. government totally bankrupt? It's through Wall Street. Wall Street is totally bankrupt. It cannot recover. It is dead. What is going to have to happen, is we're going to have to declare Wall Street to have been *dead*. And we're going to introduce a new method which is key to what Franklin Roosevelt represented, during his Presidency. It's not quite the same thing, but it's the same nature of intention.

Now, we lost everything, when Franklin Roosevelt died, because we had a series of bum Presidents; we had a few Presidents who in the meantime were alive. We had Kennedy; two Kennedys were killed. One served as President. The other was not given a chance to serve as the President; he was killed before that could happen. And over this period of time, there have been some moments of goodness, in terms of the processes of the U.S. government. But most of the time, since then, *no!* Everything has been a disaster.

We have to come to an understanding of what the solution is on this thing. And I don't think my just answering this question will settle it. I think, however, if we follow through on some of the questions that come up normally under this condition, I think we'll have a pretty good discussion.

Q: Mr. LaRouche, I am E—M— from Manhattan. On behalf of all your supporters in the Manhattan Project, I want to wish you a very happy birthday, which I guess is in two days. [Sept. 8] But I just want to say that I feel lucky to have become acquainted with you and your knowledge and purpose. And because of your dedication to keeping the planet a safe place for everyone, it has inspired me, as well to fight for the truth and the well-being of all of us, as you have.

That's all I have to say. [applause]

Threatened for Telling the Truth

LaRouche: Thank you. Thank you very much.

Q: Hello, Mr. LaRouche, nice meeting you. My name is P—. I just have one question— two questions; it's one question with two sides to it.

I was told that you were in jail for ten [sic] years for your political opinions, for your political activism. I'm not exactly sure what for—I wasn't told the whole details. But I kind of assumed that it was because you were trying to do the right thing, and someone didn't like that.

My question is, sometimes I'm afraid of expressing all of my opinions that would be truth, and that would be truthful and trying to make America a better place; and sometimes I have this fear that there's always someone watching. There's always something watching everything we say online, everything that we say in public; everything that we write, everything that we read, especially with the internet. And my question to you is, what do you make of that, and what do you think is the best way to deal with it?

LaRouche: Well, in brief, my career in business, in terms of our Federal business, is that I reached a certain point in the beginning of the 1970s, which led into my appointment to a special position, to represent a new President, Ronald Reagan. And the thing which I was entrusted to do, was to deliver a proposal for dealing with Russia, or Russia at that time, which had just lost its leading member; and we had come to an agreement which I negotiated with the Russians to ensure that there would be no war between the United States and Russia. I was the one who negotiated that, and I did other things of the same nature. I also did some things which made me very unpopular with people like the Bushes and similar kinds of people, and Obama as well.

So, the effect was—despite the fact that I was put in the jug and all these other kinds of things at a later point—that what I have stood for is valid today totally. And the whole thing that we base this,—for example, Russia is in a very crucial period. Now, Russia is not a bad nation, or something like that; China's involved.

The Chinese military parade on Sept. 3, celebrating the Chinese people's victory in the War of Resistance against Japan, and the end of World War II in the Pacific.

You had a large demonstration in China, a massive one. Something beyond the conventions of any kind.

And today we're at that point. Now, in this period, for various reasons, my aged process, which is me, has come to a point of contributing to the possible hope that we will bring the planet Earth out of the danger which has now threatened us, of a thermonuclear conflict, whose effect and probable effect will be extermination of the human species. And I'm very happy to have some role in contributing to that mission, to defeat the threat which is by Obama himself, personally; the effect which threatens the existence of the human species.

Q: [follow-up] But sometimes trying to fight that threat brings us some kind of threat to ourselves, as we could be put in a situation where we might become persecuted for trying to do the right thing.

LaRouche: That's true. But that goes with the territory. We have had a number of evil Presidents and some corrupt ones who are not just evil, but massively corrupt. We've had all kinds of things happen to the United States, and I've been fortunate enough to have had the experiences that I've had, so I'm able to respond to these matters. And you know, I've had a good life so far, and I probably will get a little more mileage out of it, if we're lucky right now. I don't think I'm going to live very long, because I'm kind of an old man. *But!* I'm determined to fight and carry out my business, and I will be content that we shall become victorious. Period.

Q: Good afternoon, Mr. LaRouche, R— from Brooklyn. I'd like to know your position on the TPP [Trans-Pacific Partnership] agreement as a provision similar to the NAFTA Chapter 7, which means that, even if we get Glass-Steagall through or passed, the multinational funds may be able to circumvent the Glass-Steagall by the right-to-profit doctrine which they have in the NAFTA Chapter 7, and in the TPP.

LaRouche: Well, the point is that Glass-Steagall, of course, first came into being, directly [under FDR]; of course, it was always implicitly there under Alexander Hamilton, who, of course, is known to people in Manhattan; his corpse is there, still, being admired by honest people.

But the issue here is Glass-Steagall. Glass-Steagall was the formulation which was provided by President Franklin Roosevelt to deal with the evil that was reigning over the United States during the 1920s, in particular. And Franklin Roosevelt created this new process, which saved the United States.

Unfortunately, actions came into effect immediately after his death, to destroy what Franklin Roosevelt had accomplished. And over the period since that time, most of the Presidencies of the United States have been heavily corrupted. The most recent Presidents, the Bush family and Obama, are the most evil things that have been imposed on the United States in history to date. And only by defeating those forces, now, can we possibly save civilization, from what is otherwise a thermonuclear conflict from which *very few human beings will survive.*

In other words, if Obama has his will, he will soon launch a thermonuclear war which will kill most of the people on the planet in one very short time. That's the danger.

Now, because we're in a period which is beyond what we've known in wars before—World War I was already bad enough; World War II was the last word. What happened, of course, in the case of our great Presidents of that time, they knew this was the case. And so since that time we've been living off and on between corrupt and evil Presidents, and evil party compositions, and trying to struggle out, and get an exception.

Under the Bush Administration and the Obama Ad-

When U.S. presidents pursued peace: FDR with Marshal Joseph Stalin at the Tehran Conference, 1943.

ministration, the thing has been brought to an endgame. Destruction of these forces is absolutely necessary. What is happening right at this moment is that China and Russia have taken an action, which, if properly carried out, will be a great contribution to prevention of the kind of holocaust, which threatens mankind right now.

Not a Jewish Question

Q: Good afternoon, Mr. LaRouche. I'm J—W— from Brooklyn, New York. Okay. My question deals with crafty, sheisty Israel. I had to draw a little map—I don't know if you can see it, but—I had to draw a little map of Syria, and put Israel where it belongs, and Jordan, and Lebanon, and you know, Turkey over here, and Iraq above Syria. I had to actually draw out a little map of that area, in order to understand the placement of these nations....

So my question is, if Israel is supporting ISIS to the north and they're also supporting ISIS to the south, and saying that they're supporting al Nusra as if al Nusra was not an actual faction of both al-Qaeda and ISIS, then what can we do, or what does Russia need to do, in order to deal with Israel, if they intend to help Syria and keep the Assad government in place and protect Damascus and the other ports that are needed in Syria? So I want to know more about this Israel thing.

LaRouche: Okay, you've come to the right address. You may be gratified.

But we have to clarify actually what we mean by

"Israel." Because during the immediate period after the post-World War II period, I became closely associated as a supporter of the Israeli military force.

Now, this force, however, which was the forces of my friends at that time, in the Israeli government; you know, this was a very tough period for Israelis and others as well. But this particular force of the leadership of Israel *then* was a great achievement coming out of what the effect was of what the Nazis had done to the Jewish population.

Now, what happened was, the British got in on this, and there was an election. And the government which came into power was under British and other influence [Menachem Begin], and that influence overwhelmed—not totally, but nearly overwhelmed—what the Israeli government had accomplished in its defense program and its reforms during that period.

So what happened was, a group based on London of Israeli interests organized chiefly in London, but also spread from London into the United States itself. So you had a Jewish population in the United States which became increasingly brainwashed, and adopted an attitude against all kinds of things, and was absolutely incompetent.

The recent government of Israel has been evil. It is purely evil as much as anything else. But during this period, there have been leaders of Israel, during this same period, who were *murdered* on behalf of the other kinds of Israelis; or imprisoned, virtually, destroyed!

So it is not a Jewish question. It's a British question. And there were certain Jewish circles, and money interests involved in that; they're bought, or they're desperate. They're told lies. They don't know what the story is. Honest Jewish people in the United States and elsewhere are like Einstein, they're good people.

Then you have a British interest comes in, and takes over the government of Israel, and turns it into a virtual criminal operation. Just like the most recent, new election in Israel, it was a *disaster* for humanity. And there's no reason for this stuff. It's evil. But it's not Jewish; it's not a Jewish question. It's a British question.

Clinton Presidential Library

When Israelis sought peace: Israeli Prime Minister Yitzhak Rabin (left) shakes hands with PLO Chairman Yasser Arafat (right) under the auspices of President William Clinton, in October 1993.

And a British question is usually also a brutish question. [laughter]

Q: Hi. My name is A— I'm an activist for this Manhattan Project now. And my question is, over the past few days I've been organizing people in New York, especially on Putin's action. There has been very strong sense of optimism that I got from people who came to the table and learned about Putin's bold assumption that we can actually defeat terrorism, and have a coalition internationally to do this.

One tendency, however, that I have found, also within myself, is to overanalyze a situation and try to explain how this initiative's going to somehow have a trickle-down effect, and how things are going to work out somehow.

But it's my hypothesis that we have to use this bold assumption coming from Putin, and also Xi Jinping of China,—an optimism that humanity can overcome the greatest threat that we are facing as mankind, and use this as a kind of an inspiration; meaning that, not only do we have to explain to people here what's going on, but it seems to me that we here in New York have to respond to this inspiration from the United States. Of course, that means 25th Amendment and getting Obama out, passing Glass-Steagall. But my question is how can we have this sort of mass effect—not in a way that we explain things, but how can we actually move the population, given what China and Russia have done?

At the Brink of Change

LaRouche: Well, I don't think the problem is that difficult. I think the only difficulty is getting the job done in a timely fashion. Because you will notice now that there are directions and trends in the United States and in parts of Europe, where the whole system that had been dominating the trans-Atlantic period, is now collapsing. That political system is now collapsing.

You saw a reflection of this in what happened in China recently, and what's happened in Russia, and other things. What's happened in Asia. You find that all of these things that the British Empire had represented for its long period of existence, are what we've seen in the Presidency of the United States under the two sets of skunks—a Bush skunk and an Obama skunk—which have occupied virtually four terms of the Presidential office.

So that mainly, no young person in the United States knows what a human being is, because they haven't met one yet. It's true! They don't know any better. Look inside the United States, what do you see? In Hollywood, what do you see in the United States, what do you see on the streets, what do you see as habits? You think, "This is the United States?!" This is not a United States; it's a disease!

And what's happening? Well, diseases sometimes get cured. And what's happening now, is, we have a movement inside the United States, which, if you measure things carefully, as weeks go by, you find there are trends now which are moving *against* this kind of evil.

But that does not mean we can sit there and just wait for victory. But it does mean that the American people, or a good part of them, and especially in New York City,—there are lots of people in New York City, not the majority, perhaps, but in New York, you see a different kind of person. And they're trying to scratch, and find out what the answers are.

No, but we have to have confidence in the fact that their humanity, has a profoundly underlying good view, or at least has had in modern history. And therefore, you have to count on that, but you don't count on it by looking at it. You've got to get out there and help promote it. And if you promote the kind of things that people are capable of, then we can win. And I would say now that what's happening, particularly with what Putin and China have just done, has actually brought us to the

kremlin.ru

Russian President Vladimir Putin speaking at the first Eastern Economic Forum in Vladivostok Sept. 4. He addressed plans for developing the Far East, and the importance of the Sept. 3 military parade and celebration in Beijing, which he attended, as a sign of the commitment of THE nations attending to ensure that fascism never arises again.

brink, of reversing the evil which has menaced us, under the Bush family and under Obama. These things can be removed. It's going to take a little bit of *nudging* to make sure that that change occurs.

Q: Lyn, hi. This is M— from Manhattan. [sings] "Happy birthday to you." [laughter]

You know, I have to tell you, back in 1998, I was so dismayed after teaching a day of class in science, and this and that. I have three questions. And I was standing in my kitchen, yelling at my skylight: "I want the truth, Buddha! What the hell is going on?" And I had three questions. My son's 15 years of age, and he's sitting there going, "Ma, you're crazy."

And I said, "My God, I'm late for the post office," and I got out there at the post office and there were your guys. The three questions were answered for me, so ever since I've been working with you. And I had an education in Flushing, Queens from the Catholic school and the nuns. I believed in the United States of America and the goodness of mankind. Even though I'm now a Buddhist, there's the goodness of mankind. Within each human being is the essence of absolute goodness, compassion, and compassionate action, that's the thing, action based on wisdom....

You know, of course, I always associated so much of my information as from the LaRouche organization and what we have done. When Benjamin Franklin said, "you lose the press, you've lost the Republic," and this is what we are now in danger of.

And I know, just as the young gal who spoke ahead of me, when you mention Putin's name, they look at you as if he's some sort of a criminal....

I will say one thing. I called up, I think, Senator Schumer and I said to the fellow that answered the phone, "You've got to face it. This President ain't no Christian. He's a Wahhabi Muslim. He's those same guys that were on the planes that went into the building on 9/11! This guy's holding hands with the watchamacallit of Saudi Arabia...." "Oh!" he said, "no, no, no"; he got so upset at the thought that Obama is really deep in his heart no Christian. He is a crazy, radicalized, murderous Muslim! And not my kind of Muslim friend, you know, because I want you to know I have nothing against the Muslim religion.

But what can we do, coming up, to somehow or other in the next week-and-a-half make this clear to the American people, that they have to stand against the President and get him out?

Often You're Fighting Yourself

LaRouche: [laughs] That's a good point here. I think what you're saying, is something which I understand very well. It's, that if you want to become successful in influencing other people, you've got to commit yourself to the mission which does that.

And when you're talking with people,—it's like ordinary family and community discussions,—these discussions reflect something. Some people will say, "Yes, perhaps you're right, but I don't think you're right. I think they're right. I think you have to learn to keep your head low, and don't take any leadership roles that might embarrass you or embarrass your neighbors." And therefore what happens is that their good intentions are no longer good intentions, because if something is *right*, and you know it's right, and you have evidence that it's right, you don't dump it.

The typical American, today, especially those young people today, two generations or so, they're degenerations: Look at the culture of most of our young people. Look at Californication, since Schwarzenegger got in on this mess, and brought Satan there, to other places, huh? This kind of thing.

So the point is, it's your own devotion from inside

Mankind's function is to contribute to the advancement of humanity. Here, Dutch Renaissance artist Johannes Vermeer's depiction of The Geographer.

you, to have a mission-orientation, which is appropriate and relevant, and is something that *will not let you go.* When you get to that point, someone says, "Well, you know, but that's not practical. That's not practical."

"Well," I say, "maybe your life is not practical." Maybe you should change the course. Maybe you as a human being, have an obligation, to make a contribution to the advancement of a function of humanity. You have to defend humanity as a principle. Don't sit on the sidelines and say "It's not practical. It's not practical."

It has to be practical. Because what do we have? We have a situation, where we don't have a real economy in the United States any more. We don't have it! It's been destroyed. What happened? Well we had a couple of degenerations, a Bush degeneration and an Obama degeneration, making about four terms of Presidential office; and this is what has destroyed us. This is what has done it to us. We didn't have the *guts*, or many of us didn't have the guts, to fight against this. And, what you're fighting for is not fighting against someone; you're often fighting against yourself. You're fighting against yourself, so you don't become a skunk like the guy in the neighborhood was.

Q: [follow-up] All right, yes! That's got it. You've got it. Happy birthday, Lyn [laughter, applause]

Q: Hi, Lyn, it's A—. I wanted to talk with you about what is now, I think, the Nero effect of Obama being on full display, with every nation now, and all the reports coming in on how nations are being destroyed, one by one,—Syria, Ukraine, Libya, and so forth. The Green policy that Obama embraces. He's entertaining the murderers and accomplices and partners of the British in the White House, while all these events are unfolding. And here comes Putin now to intervene on a military basis, strategically, to counter the destruction of Syria.

I wanted to know from you what is your analysis of that intervention? And how can this help to offset this global drive for destruction that Obama sits by and allows to occur?

LaRouche: Okay, a couple of weeks ago I presented a case to some of my associates and others on the question of the policy of Putin. I also followed that immediately, this past week, of course, with what China had done with its demonstration. Now, from a military standpoint, when you see this marching among the China organization; these were general officers, generally, and you would have these swarms of China's military specialists, and there were actually general officers commanding what would normally be a regiment. But they're out there setting a pace which I have never seen the like of before.

The way in which that march, which was done this past week, that march by these soldiers, by these officers, was absolutely amazing. In the records of military science and drill, there's been nothing like that, in any part of history, recently. It's amazing!

But then you see the end of the thing; they go through the process, the whole march process, which itself is a military miracle; but we understand how it was done. But now we turn up with this whole weapons system China has. It's amazing. It's first rate! And that's only the obvious stuff.

The Coming World System

So you have a situation now where China has now mobilized itself together with Russia, to change the course of history, in general, very seriously. And Putin

has, in this same context, I was going through this thing and of running estimates of what Putin was going to do, and I came to a conclusion; and I found out recently that I was totally right in my conclusion: Putin is moving by proper approaches of strategy, he is moving to move forces inside their neighbors, and it's going to move. And Obama is going to scream; and Obama is going to blow, because he will not stand for what Putin is trying to do now.

And I think Obama is going to lose. That's a fact. But that's a fact which is of the type which is a possible fact, a feasible fact. That depends on the next stage, which is of actual fact, an efficient fact.

You know, war has changed since I had military experience in wartime. It's changed. It was changed by what happened with MacArthur. See, MacArthur had beaten Japan. But what happened is, the Presidency of the United States launched thermonuclear war against two cities of Japan. And since that time the possibility of thermonuclear war has been on the table.

MacArthur was totally against it and did everything possible to prevent it. Other generals of our command did the same kind of thing. They had the same kind of attitude, but you'll find that the skunks in the electorate, the skunks are the ones who create those kinds of wars.

We've come to a time in history, when general warfare as it has been defined before, in the various wars in the Nineteenth Century, Twentieth Century; this kind of warfare is no longer possible. Because the weapons of warfare, thermonuclear weapons of warfare and similar kinds of warfare, are such that you cannot have *general warfare* without rushing into killing most of the human species.

So Obama, and the Bushes are killers; the supporters of evil, the Saudis. The Saudis are a British agent, which is a matter of pure evil. The Bush Presidency was a full supporter of that evil. We had some people in New York City and elsewhere who were killed by Saudis; and the Saudis did it, under the orders of the British, and I know a lot of the details of how that happened and how that worked.

So we've come to this kind of a period. Obama is a stooge, but he's an evil stooge. Bush was a fool, President Bush. President Obama is an evil force; and if you cater to him, you'll get an evil force. Because Obama is prepared now, if he can get by with it, to launch a full-scale thermonuclear attack on Russia and other places. Such a launch, which will be responded to by Russia, would virtually exterminate most of the human popula-

Nations are coming together globally to present an alternative to mankind. Here, the leaders of the BRICS hold a working breakfast on July 9, 2015 at their summit in Ufa, Russia.

Mankind's Mission

The difference is, we are all going to die as human beings. We can't live on forever. We won't live on forever. So what's the meaning of human life? If we're all going to die, what is the meaning and the virtue of human life?

The fact is, we are able to contribute discoveries of principle, in the course of our work, to enrich our people in terms of their capabilities of creativity. And mankind therefore lives, yes, in order to die. But, what does that mean, in order to die in those terms? It means you are fulfilling the span of your mortal life, and that you are devoting your life to making contributions to the *future of mankind*, scientific discoveries, new, real great ones.

Kepler discovered the characteristics of the system. He did it. We now know there is a higher form, the Galactic System. We know that we have to master the Galactic System, which is our water supply; mankind's water supply is located in the Galaxy, the major part of it. We have to develop those things in it. China is engaged now in many things, in space programs which are of this nature.

So, the point is, mankind has a mission which no other living species has ever had. The ability to serve the Creator, through service of what we call scientific and related discoveries, great artistic discoveries, moral discoveries. The idea of the principle of God, a principle to which we are indebted. And what we must do is use that capability which is given to us, to enable mankind to go through successive generations of birth and death, but in the process, to always bring mankind into discoveries of principle which mankind had never known before.

Mankind is the only truly immortal, living being that we know. And mankind's job is to have performed a *mortal achievement*, which brings forth capabilities of mankind, scientific and other related things, which have never been known before. And our devotion to

tion, *within a day.*

So we've come to that kind of situation. And warfare as we've known it before, or as MacArthur knew it in his service in Europe, that's no longer possible. That kind of warfare is no longer possible. Because thermonuclear war makes it impossible, and other kind of weapons system makes it impossible.

We've now come to the point where the relations among nations have to be changed: nations must come to a moral standard of productivity, of creativity, of rising to higher achievements; of exploring space, developing the galaxy, which is an essential task before us in the times to come. So, it's a new period. And therefore the important thing is to mobilize the population of the United States, of Germany, of Russia, of China,—and China and Russia are very much on this case right now.

We have to bring those forces together. Because we are not going to go on the old kind of national system, because the national system cannot be based on warfare, not modern warfare. There have to be other kinds of alternatives. And some parts of the world are seeing that, they're seeing that change. Because, what's the purpose of mankind? What is mankind? Well, the idiots don't know what mankind is. Mankind is a superior being. There is no form of animal life which can match the principle of the human being.

that purpose, gives us, anyone, when they die, or are about to die, and they say "This has been the good fight." Because in the course our life we produce something *new* for mankind, which brings mankind to a higher levels of achievement for a mission which mankind can never fully appreciate, but which is the mission which inspires people to a purpose, which is the real true meaning of humanity.

No animal species is immortal. Only mankind is immortal in terms of mankind's ability to create new conditions in the Universe from which mankind will advance to higher levels. Just as Kepler went up and discovered the Solar System, we now have discovered the Galactic System. And we don't know how far or where that is going to work out. But we know that mankind has a destiny, a sacred destiny, to achieve *insight* into what mankind can learn to create. And that's the way to look at it.

Mankind is not just an animal. Mankind is something far better, far richer, far more important. And we should aspire to be an example of that. [Applause.]

Q: [follow-up] Lyn, I just wanted to follow up. I mentioned early on, in first talking with you now about Obama and this Nero condition, clinical condition, that it's been over six years since you hauled that out. And it's typical amongst these types of cases that their condition only worsens, never gets better, and becomes more and more dangerous. So, for over six years he's been qualified to be removed from office by means of the 25th Amendment. But I don't think we're really thinking in those terms, but rather more like it being some kind of a tactic, as opposed to like our very lives depend on it.

LaRouche: [laughs]. Well, I don't accept that condition, you know. I think that we are responsible,—collectively, if not individually,—we're responsible to find a solution to these problems, this kind of threat.

Look, it's been done before. The founding of the United States, even before that,—Alexander Hamilton, for example, is a case of this thing. And his corpse is living down at the tip of Manhattan there still today. He still is the exemplary standard of devotion to service for mankind. He was the guy that got George Washington to run for President. George Washington was not going to do it otherwise. He did it.

So we had a British agent who came in and killed him, because he refused to lift a gun against a citizen of the United States. So he was murdered, slaughtered, by

an evil man.

There's No Excuse

Now the problem is, we have the access to knowledge. Now I've lived through this thing, I know what's there, I know the failures of the United States, and the failures of the trans-Atlantic community. *These failures are not necessary. They were never necessary.* It was only the weakness of the people who lacked the development, and lacked the passion, to realize what mankind's destiny is.

And we've had great people, in the Nineteenth Century, great achievers, and we've lost this quality of achievement. We had it with Franklin Roosevelt. Franklin Roosevelt gave us this kind of policy. The general officers who commanded service in World War II were typical of those people who performed an essential service, which they didn't like, but they had to do.

And we had the murder of great Presidents, or the assassinations of people who were almost great Presidents, who were part of this thing. There is no excuse for accepting this kind of condition. I will never accept it. I cannot accept it. I never will. And the best I can do is to try to encourage some other people not to do it either. [Applause]

Q: Hi, Mr. LaRouche, this E—B— from the Bronx. First of all, I want to wish you a very happy birthday next Tuesday.

I would like to ask you what is your opinion about Senator Bernie Sanders. He's also running for President, and he's against the rich corporations. He would want them to not get away with tax loopholes, and he's fighting for the poor class, and the working class, and the middle class. He's a Democrat and a Socialist. I would like to know, do you think he would make a much better President than Obama?

LaRouche: [laughs] That's not even fair to the voter! Obama is a bum. He should be removed at any time.

Q: [follow-up] Also the Glass Steagall. He [Sanders] supports the Glass-Steagall. So, what is your impression of him, your opinion about him?

LaRouche: I think he's probably not the strongest Presidential candidate. Right now he has a certain degree of popularity coming out of where he lives. But there are others.

The way I put the thing: The idea that you have to

have *a* President as such, and that that President alone is the Presidency of the United States, that, in fact, is a mistake. There have been great Presidents of the United States. Franklin Roosevelt was a great President, for example.

But the idea is, if you want to have a Presidential system, the first thing is you don't want to have a one-only President; because a one-only President is too easy a target to kill, among other things. And therefore what you want on that kind of lesson and warning, what you want, is you want to have an assembly with a President, who is a President, and the leading figure of the United States government. But then you want a whole team of people, who, with their assorted capabilities put together, represent a government. But they have to be people who are committed to that service. Now Franklin Roosevelt was pretty successful in that respect.

Other cases are not. Look at what happened to Kennedy. John F. Kennedy actually saved the United States from a thermonuclear war. Kennedy did it! And what did he get paid for it? He was assassinated. What did he get? There was his brother. Then his brother was assassinated, because the brother could have actually become President. He was also assassinated.

The President I served, they tried to assassinate him, Reagan. I was part of the official team of Ronald Reagan's government. And that's one of the reasons I got sent to prison. Because I did things the Bush family didn't like.

The point is, these are the facts that have to be dealt with: we need to have a composition of people who comprise a real U.S. government, who have the talents to do that, who have the devotion to serve in that way. This would be something like a Franklin Roosevelt government, because that's what the Franklin Roosevelt government tended to be. Roosevelt was very careful of this stuff, and that's what we need.

So I think the answer is, we need a Presidential system, and I think we might have one or two people; or one, two, or others, who would be a leading President, ahead of the official President. But we need a *team*, which is a team which represents the kind of knowledge, interplay of knowledge, which qualifies a government, a Presidential administration to cover, shall we say, the ground of what has to be considered in, say two terms of a Presidency, or more. That's what we need.

FDR Library

Franklin Delano Roosevelt mobilizes New Yorkers on October 31, 1936, during his re-election campaign rally at Madison Square Garden. Shown from left: FDR, Governor Herbert Lehman, and Senator Robert F. Wagner.

Get Rid of Wall Street

I don't think the Sanders thing is crucial. I think he's a useful person; he's running for office now. O'Malley is also a more active one, but he has less voting popularity at the moment.

But so what we need is a Presidential *system*, which is composed of people who are qualified to fill the various duties and tasks which a Presidency requires. And you need to have some kind of protection so you don't have one guy out there, or two guys out there, who are both vulnerable to assassination, the way Kennedy and his brother were assassinated.

Remember, *Kennedy saved the United States from thermonuclear extermination in the Cuba crisis.* He organized it. His brother was a key agent in assisting that. They were both murdered. Why were they murdered? Because there was a contrary force of evil which deliberately assassinated them, and I think we had a famous leader of the FBI who played very significant role in bringing that about.

Q: Good afternoon, Mr. LaRouche, this is Mr. C— from New York. I have two questions I want to ask. The first one is, can the passing of Glass-Steagall stimulate the economy immediately? And what would be the first shovel-ready project to start on? Would it be NAWAPA, infrastructure, agriculture or nuclear power plants, fission or fusion? And the second question is, how on earth can we get other people involved in organizing instead of being bystanders? Do you have any suggestions?

LaRouche: Yes, sure. We don't need that. We don't need to worry about that kind of stuff. I think we can pull it off, right now. I think there's a mood now in the U.S. population. You know, most of our people are poorly educated. I mean, most of our young people aren't fit to be educated; they're too busy doing other things that are not going to take us anywhere important. But no, the issue here is, we do have a policy. It's called Glass-Steagall; it's the Franklin Roosevelt policy.

But, here's the problem. The problem is that we don't have the kind of leadership actively now, which we need to carry out a Glass-Steagall policy. That is, we could, with a good election process, immediately, create a Glass-Steagall system. We could do it. We could get the United States out of the bankruptcy.

But then the problem is this: most of the people who are employed in the United States, or would be employed if they were able to do it, are incompetent. Look at the condition of skills of our labor force. These young people are not competent. The kinds of things they like to do, are the worst things you should ever want to do. You have a minimum number of people who really want to do something right, in terms of productivity and skills, but they don't have the chance to do it. We don't have a program for that.

So it means we need a combination of, on the one hand, a Glass-Steagall law, *period, absolutely*. There's no way you can't accept it. That means you've got to wipe out *Wall Street*. Because Wall Street is impossibly bankrupt. Wall Street is complete fraud. It's more than a complete fraud. It's past death. Right now. There's no way that the Wall Street banking system could survive, unless it took the people with them, into death.

So we have to do something about getting rid of the Wall Street crowd. And Wall Street and what it represents must be thrown out of office now. If you don't do that, there's no chance of solving the problem.

On the other hand, we have people who don't have the skills, didn't get the skills, didn't get the education and skills, to be able to do this kind of work. So there-

AIP/Niels Bohr Library

It takes real science education to create a competent population. Exemplary of competent educators was German scientist Carl Friedrich Gauss (1777-1855).

fore, we have to have a program of reconstruction of the U.S. economy which corrects these errors. We've got to get people educated competently. We have young people who are not competent. You know, at your age, and so forth, you know what this is about. We don't have the competent people. And what people who could be competent are not being educated, aren't being backed up. We don't have a productive process now. We're being destroyed, and I think we could solve the problem.

But we're going to have to move quickly; we're going to have to take a Franklin Roosevelt approach. Glass-Steagall, *yes*, primarily. But what are we going to do to make Glass-Steagall work? We can do Glass-Steagall; we should do it, immediately. How are we going to make it work? I know something we can do about it. But that has to be what's on the subject.

We've got a lot of people in the United States, who just are completely lacking in all real skills or they're downgraded skills, which don't mean much of anything. The education system stinks. This is terrible. Yes, if you and I and some other people are angry enough about this thing, in the right way, I think we could organize something. We just have to be given the latitude to do something about it. Which is simply a matter of leadership. You've got to find people who are determined to be successful leaders. I mean this happened, for example, in history of Abraham Lincoln. Suddenly we got a bunch of people who had been slaves, and suddenly a number of them turned out to be geniuses. That's the way you have to look at it. And if Abraham Lincoln had lived longer, then everything else would have lived longer.

The Mobilization We Need

Q: Hi, Mr. LaRouche, this is R—, from Bergen County, New Jersey. My question to you is, what is wrong with the EU? [laughter] Are they a bunch of morally corrupt degenerates, or is it the case that they really don't have two nickels to rub together? Because, this thing, this entity, this freak show, that is labelled as the EU is aiding and abetting some of the most outrageous criminal atrocities, ever imaginable with the refugee stuff going on. These are war crimes. And these people who have been through major wars don't seem to even have it within them, to be able to accommodate taking care of a million or so people.

There seems to be something hugely wrong with this entity called the EU. It looks to me like it really should be broken up. It is a complete failure. First, there was the Greek thing; now there's the refugee thing. Isn't it a disaster? What would you say on this topic?

LaRouche: Of course it is. But I think we could do something about it, we can do something about it. I think if we just extend our capabilities now, and get some teamwork going, I think we can do it.

Obviously, Manhattan is one of the areas—I mean, we know what Manhattan is. We know what the sins of Manhattan are. We know what some of the talent is of Manhattan, now—education, science, so forth, to the degree that exists. Yes. If we want to, we could get the people rousted up to do the right thing.

You have to have the infectious drive, doing that. Most of my life has been spent on doing exactly that kind of thing, and I've found out that I could succeed, unless they really tried to kill me. And we don't have enough people who are doing that kind of fighting, they have lost their ambition.

You know, they would say, "be practical." Did you ever hear someone say, "Hey, come on, be practical, be practical, be practical?" Wasn't that cry to being practical, not to offend unpleasant people, or something like that? That's the problem.

The problem, is you've got to get the American people to come together in sufficient degree that they have a sense of a *mission* in life, not a career, but a *mission* in life; when people have a mission in life to make discoveries, to make achievements. When they just want to make money, and the problem is the American citizen is corrupted by saying, "You want to make money? You want to have a successful career? Well, shut up and be careful what you say."

What is needed is a mobilization of leading citizens or citizens who are passionate to make things happen that must happen. We did that before. We've done that before; I did it a number of times. And when you do it, it works. In prison, it doesn't work so good. But we can do it.

I think we are on the edge of a circumstance where—you take in the New York area, I think there's something going on there now; that people are wondering, if there isn't an option to change things. Because, remember, what's going to hit Manhattan is Wall Street. *Wall Street is finished.* And Wall Street is totally bankrupt and cannot be recovered. It is exceeded beyond all possibility of bailout. The only way to do this is to cancel Wall Street.

Now what would be happening with cancelling Wall Street? Well, suddenly Wall Street would be shut down, because there's no value in it. It's a complete fraud. But people are afraid because Wall Street controls money. It controls money in banks; it controls money in other kinds of institutions. People say, "Well, I need a career, I need an income." "What are you going to do, take my income away from me? Shut it down? You're going to take Wall Street away from me? I depend on Wall Street. Look, I have a brother-in-law who has a career in accounting here and there. You want to take his job away from him?" Or do you want to say, "Joe, stop being a jerk. What's your skill? What do you know?"

And the problem is people get sucked into popular opinion, and I'm an advocate of *unpopular opinion*, and I think that's the right career to have.

Throw Obama Out of Office

Q: Hi, Lyn, this is D— in New York. I just want to consider what's going to happen over the next few weeks in New York, as the United Nations General Assembly begins, in the context of what you're saying is coming from Russia and China. Because, it's funny, for example, that all of these Presidents that are going to come into New York, and heads of state and government, and a few days ago, Russia took over as President of the United Nations Security Council. So, Putin's going to be here, and he's going to be like the President of all the Presidents in New York City, which I think is pretty ironic.

So therefore, these actions to be taken by Russia and

China in the lead-up to what's happening here, I was reading in this week's *EIR*, some of the article by your associate Mike Steger, about Franklin Roosevelt's First Hundred Days. And he emphasizes in his conclusion the relationship between Roosevelt and Shelley. And considering that we have this moment that has never occurred, for this 70th anniversary of the creation of the UN by FDR, I mean, my question is, what would Percy Shelley do, in this moment, in New York?

LaRouche: I don't think that's a legitimate question. Because, look at what the situation is. Right now, Wall Street is bankrupt: That means the entire banking system of the United States, of the Wall Street banking, is hopelessly bankrupt. It's gone beyond all possibility of bankruptcy. Hmm?

So, now, on the other side, we have an issue, where Russia and China, under threats from Obama, in particular, are faced with a war, thermonuclear war. Obama is now committed, to launching thermonuclear war!

Now, what's happened of course, is that Putin and China, and other nations, have made a pact, in effect, now, to throw Obama effectively out of office. So therefore, going out with neat plans, schemes, is not the answer. The principle of the flank goes to rank; we have to shut down Wall Street. Wall Street is hopelessly bankrupt! The United States cannot function under a Wall Street regime. It's worthless! Absolutely worthless. What do you do? You shut down Wall Street, which was done against Hoover by Franklin Roosevelt. Shut it down!

Now, the problem here, today, is *worse* than Franklin Roosevelt faced in his election, when he was made President. So, you can't take a model, and say, this is the model and this model and that model, or whatever, will work. You've got to be much more practical than that: You've got to sense exactly what can be done, and I think what's happened right now, what I know has happened, because I went through this thing: that Putin's suddenly made a change of his operation. And he moved into Syria, and he moved in to defend Syria against what? Against whom? Against the forces of evil. So therefore, the action against the forces of evil which is coming on right now, is coming on from China; it's coming on from Putin; and so forth. And there are

Xinhua

A new international framework: Here Chinese Premier Li Keqiang (left) meeting with his Russian counterpart Dmitri Medvedev in Moscow, Oct. 13, 2014.

other forces like that, same thing. Same center.

So there's something already in process, and it's the question of whether that process will continue successfully or not, which is going to determine, already, what the fight is of humanity for the immediate period head. It's already been established.

In other words, the idea that we can go out with a scheme, and this scheme by itself is going to provide the answer to the alternative we desire, history does not work that way. You have to make history. And what I'm saying: The Wall Street case, Wall Street is hopelessly bankrupt! There's no way that Wall Street can survive! It's beyond all possibility of salvation; it's going to collapse.

Now, what are you going to do about the Wall Street collapse? Are you going to be able to go in, and say, "shut down Wall Street"? "We're going to establish a new banking system." Replace that? We can do that. Well, that's what we have to do. We can do that!

What we need right now is a Presidential candidacy which will move in that direction. I think there are a couple of people in that process, who typify what can be brought to bear, because the nation is going to have to face the reality: "Wall Street is dead!" It's gone beyond the possibility of its continued life. If you don't do something about it, you're going to cause the worst kind of disaster that mankind can possibly have: So therefore, we have to *act* to get rid of that problem. Put it into mercy death,—that is, Wall Street as such. There's no way you can bail it out; there's no way you can salvage it. It's gone.

And we have international capabilities in terms of nations, like China, India, Russia, and so forth, other nations who can be taught to behave themselves, and get us out of this problem.

So we have to take the situation, not with a scheme, but we have to take the situation and say: What does the situation demand of us?

Our Devotion

Q: A blessed afternoon to you, sir! We have a President who is beyond description; we all agree on that. I have two questions to you. One, I realize he would do anything to hold onto power, which I don't think he's going to be able to do; but he may do some struggles in that direction and I was wondering what you thought we have to look forward to, and possibly prevent from the White House as Obama tries to hold onto power, and change the country as much as possible, before he leaves? That's my first question.

LaRouche: I would say, you know, this kind of thing is absolutely necessary. You have to come out with positive, creative contributions, to the benefit of mankind. You know, like Nicholas of Cusa! Here was a person who was a brilliantly modest man, that is, personally. And you get examples like that, and you find that these kinds of people, who take that view and vow in life, have been the people who have *created* the kind of culture of modern civilization. Yes, sure, in the following year, after he died, terrible things happened in Europe.

But then, the same spirit still exists, and that spirit is the one which led us into all the achievements that the United States in particular has given. And the greatest men and women in society have always had that quality. It's a not self-serving, it's serving mankind; the idea of a devotion that mankind *needs* direction, and to solve the problems that mankind faces. And those who can do that and can contribute to that, they are absolutely necessary.

And we have to, if we can, become part of that kind of devotion. We have to have a devotion in ourselves, which compels us to see that we have a mission that's given to us, a mission for the future, a mission for a new quality of mankind.

Q: [follow-up] The next question I have for you is kind of a humorous one: Elections in the United States, and you're a student of history, you know some greatly in the past, over a 100 years ago, were extremely colorful! That we have had in the past, we have had some very colorful elections. Recently, some of them have been a lot duller.

Right now, I think we're getting into a more interesting one; I think, where you've got large numbers of candidates on one side, the whole thing, is fun to watch. I wanted to know where *you* think it's going? And where you think it should go?

LaRouche: I actually am persuaded that I have a mission to perform. And that mission is to try to get people to understand what they have to do, and that's the best shot I know about. I've gone through a lot of experience; and I found out, I've made a number of discoveries, scientific discoveries, other kinds of discoveries, other kinds of things. And I find that my function is what I can contribute to mankind's ability to solve mankind's problems.

Q: [follow-up] [inaudible] has been leading us to be doing that for thousands of years. And you'd get a kick out of it: I was telling some friends earlier that I go to about the closest place to Hell, once a month to lead prayers. A group of us lead prayers in the New Jersey Statehouse! And that's about as close to Hell as you're going to get on this planet!

LaRouche: [guffaws] Sehr gut! Very good!

Speed: So, Lyn, we're now at the conclusion again. I think this week's dialogue has poised us very well for what's about to occur, what we're going into here in Manhattan. You're going to summarize anyway, but one of the things that certainly keeps occurring,—and you hear it in many of the questions today,—is how the idea of courage, and the idea of intelligence, are one and the same thing. It's an interesting thing, because Diane, of course, in the solfège, but also just in the general music discussion we're dealing with, before we come to you, this is one of the implicit matters that you're always hearing. You're always hearing it actually in the Furtwängler and other performances, that this idea of courage and intelligence is *one thing*.

And when you were answering someone saying to you, "listen, I'm scared. We have all these things to be scared of," and you said, "Yes, well, that comes with the territory. That's like, what we do."

So, I'd just like you to give a summary, recognizing that we're going to be poised to go into a real acceleration in the next few days.

If we're all going to die, what is the meaning and the virtue of human life? The fact is, we are able to contribute discoveries of principle, in the course of our work, to enrich our people in terms of their capabilities of creativity. And mankind therefore lives, yes, in order to die. But what does that mean, in order to die in those terms? It means you are fulfilling the span of your mortal life, and that you are devoting your life to making contributions to the future of mankind, scientific discoveries, new, real great ones.

Mankind is Unique

LaRouche: Well, I'll give a short explanation of what I think that means: First of all, mankind is unique. No animal is a product of mankind, it's different.

You know, what happened is, you have all these forms of life, living processes, which we can trace in ancient history and so forth, and the origins of mankind and mankind's development. But most of these things, while they were useful, more or less useful in their occurrence, were always, in one sense, failures. Even our puppy dog is a failure. Because, why? Because they're not human.

Well, what's that mean, "they're not human"? That means that mankind represents a being which is unique, to our knowledge. The idea of a Creator, of course, is a very important part of this thing, but it's very difficult to reach the idea of who the Creator is; yeah, you can understand what you mean by mean that. But you can't go out there and say, "I'm Mr. Creator's cousin," or something like that, that doesn't quite work.

So therefore, the point is, mankind is the only species which has a kind of devotion to the progress of the human species, the only species which has that devotion, to create a higher order of knowledge than mankind has ever known before. And the major thing in life for mankind, is to make a discovery, or to make a succession of discoveries which actually are new; that is, they never have been known before.

For example, let's take the case of Johannes Kepler, who discovered the Solar System. He didn't do it by any deductive methods; he did it by an insight. And now we have the Galactic System, today. We know the Galactic System is superior to this process.

And therefore, we realize that mankind is a different kind of creature. Mankind is the only creature which is intrinsically immortal. Yes, we die. But what we have done is immortal: that's the point. So you're looking at the idea of a Creator out there, some place, and the Creator is inspiring people to become creative, that is, to make discoveries which mankind has never shared before.

And that's the best thing we can do. We do as far and as well as we can. I've had a lot of experience with this sort of thing, and I can tell you, from my knowledge, that's exactly the way it works: You get on the inside of history, when you find out you think there's nothing. I've gotten that often in my scientific work; you often get to a barrier where you think, "Hmm! We've reached the limit. We don't have any way of knowing anything new beyond that." And then, if you go and do hard work and so forth, you find out, "yes, I was wrong. I was wrong. I did have a new discovery, a new principle of discovery."

And that's what makes mankind, mankind. It's that mankind—you know, Kepler is this. Nicholas of Cusa was an example of the same thing, exactly the same kind of principle: The ability to see beyond the future of mankind into what mankind can *now*, next, achieve. And it's that kind of spiritual power which is expressed in people who have that power, and I've shared that power, made a number of discoveries. So, I'm very satisfied that this works.

The problem is, we haven't educated enough people, stimulated enough people, to understand what creativity is. To them, creativity is a word, it's a word which is favored, or not, but what you have to do, is, you have to devote your life, to the purpose, as long as you can live, and never stop doing it,—what, one thing: always make a new discovery, which is valid for mankind. And when you've gotten that done, go looking for the next one.

And somewhere in the process of life, old people, for example, will die; but if they die wisely, they will die by uttering a discovery which enhances mankind's future. [applause]

Speed: I want to thank you, very, very much for that, Lyn, on behalf of everybody here. And we're going to get to work, and we'll see you, definitely, next week. [laughter]

LaRouche: OK. I won't be a phantom!

On the Death of Amelia Platts Boynton Robinson

Sept. 3—Amelia left us at the proud age of 104. Until very shortly before her death on Aug. 26, she was in full possession of her faculties, brimming as always with her passionate love for humanity and the idea that "God still has plenty for you to do"—a maxim of her life that she never gave up, whether in the famous freedom march from Selma to Montgomery on March 7, 1965, "Bloody Sunday," during which Amelia was beaten and left for dead by police on the Edmund Pettus Bridge, or when she nearly drowned in a river but survived, even though she couldn't swim, only because she was unswervingly dedicated to her mission.

Already in the 1930s, she was one of the initiators of the civil rights movement, perhaps the most important one, as it was she who started the registration of African-American voters, and especially women. And this was when the conditions prevailed that were almost the same as during the time of slavery. In view of the deep-seated racism in Alabama (among other Southern states), which prevails there to this day, and the very definite danger posed by the Ku Klux Klan, what she did took enormous courage and an unwavering vision of the true identity of mankind. Along with her husband, Samuel William Boynton, she brought many of the leaders of the movement to Selma, including James Bevel, the first who called for the march to Montgomery, Hosea Williams, and

EIRNS/Pia Maelzer

Amelia Boynton Robinson and Helga Zepp-LaRouche, in 2007.

Martin Luther King. She offered them her house as a base of operations.

The film "Selma," which was released last year, and in which Amelia is indeed represented, did not do justice to her groundbreaking importance. She herself told me, during our last meeting in Philadelphia in April, that another film about the beginnings of the civil rights movement must be made, which emphasizes the crucial role of African-American women, without which the movement never would have existed.

I met Amelia back in the early 1980s in Virginia, in the context of my husband Lyndon LaRouche's collaboration with many American civil rights activists. She was an extraordinary person of great magnetism, who was instantly able to lift her interlocutor to a higher plane of history. She saw the Schiller Institute as the continuation of the civil rights movement, and contributed to its work from 1984 to 2009 as vice president, through numerous international tours, speeches, and interventions.

Our relationship became more intense when Amelia, in March and April 1990—i.e., immediately after the peaceful revolution in Germany and in the transitional period of German reunification—visited Cottbus, Zwickau, Chemnitz, Sondershausen, Worbis, Heiligenstadt, Crivitz, and other cities. She bolstered the courage of the people there through many speeches, showing the parallels between the American civil rights movement and the one underway in Germany at that time. In this turbulent period of German history, she contributed her unique ability as a poet—with her poems and stories about Martin Luther King, as well as with beautifully performed Spirituals. Addressing people in the regions that were being transformed from the G.D.R. (East Germany) into the new federal states of reunified Germany, she made them conscious of the eternal human principles that link all those who have fought for freedom, human. and civil rights—across all times, nations, and cultures. In those exhilarating days, we adopted one another as mother and daughter.

International Impact

For 25 years, Amelia worked with the Schiller Institute as its vice president and with the Civil Rights Solidarity Movement in Germany, and often visited Sweden, Denmark, France, Italy, Germany, India, Iran, Jordan, Egypt, and, of course, countless cities in the United States itself. She always stressed the importance of love for humanity, peace, and the Dialogue of Cultures. And the many thousands of people whom she inspired to think about mankind in a bigger way, reacted with gratitude at getting to know an ambassador from the "other America," especially in the period during which the series of U.S. wars based on lies became the fashion.

She condemned the Iraq War in 2003, saying, in an interview with the Italian newspaper *Confronti*: "Evil can be changed only by its opposite, the Good. That is why I am against the war, and I don't think that evil can be corrected by an even greater injustice that will kill many innocent people. . . . I am proud of what I am, I am proud of having worked with Martin Luther King from the moment when he came to Selma up to his death, and today I am proud of my collaboration with Lyndon La-Rouche, a white man, and the Schiller Institute."

And a bit later in the interview she said: "The United States was for a long time a beacon of hope for the world. . . . Unfortunately American society and democracy have been sullied by many of our political leaders, who want to see blood and more blood. Many say the war in Afghanistan served to cover up the fact that our economy is in bad shape and we have a debt of $32 trillion. . . . To attribute all of our problems to September 11 is a way of keeping the truth hidden and distracting the world's attention from our weaknesses. The United States cannot lead a fight for Justice, if it is unjust itself. It cannot lead the world to solidarity, if acts itself according to the motto 'Divide and Conquer,' and helps itself to whatever it wants from a weaker country. But those who want war against Iraq and potentially even more wars, are not the majority of the American people. Americans see with horror and shame what we are doing to other countries in what-

ever name."

In view of the imminent threat that the United States and NATO are about to incite a huge war against Russia and China, it sounds like a last testament when Amelia, in the same interview with *Confronti*, said that Europeans should refuse to support the U.S.A. and should send representatives of their national parliaments and governments to tell Washington that "their countries will not participate in this vendetta, that they will not allow the use of military bases on their territory, and that they will give no economic support for the killing."

Another Italian publication, *Buddismo e società*, published the text of a speech that Amelia gave on Sept. 28, 2002 before a thousand people at a conference in Rome. She said, among other things: "My husband said, shortly before the outbreak of the Second World War, that we were sitting on a powder keg that could explode at any time. Today, I have the same feeling. Therefore, we must absolutely act, not only to prevent the war against Iraq, but also to avoid all the other wars that could follow from it. Today it is Iraq, tomorrow it could be Pakistan, North Korea, Vietnam, and may soon even your own country. . . . Do not allow yourselves to be corrupted, do not allow them to force upon you NATO bases for waging this war."

In her report on the civil rights movement in the United States, Amelia compared the African-Americans who at that time were afraid to become independent farmers, with those people who today are willing to accept the war: "They [these African-Americans] did not come up with the idea on their own, because they had been indoctrinated for centuries. They thought they would always have to work for their masters, just as many today are indoctrinated and think that if Bush wants war, then America has to wage war."

Amelia's immediate social milieu was dazzled at the beginning by Obama as the first African-American President, just as were countless Europeans, such as the 200,000 people who frenetically celebrated Obama in 2008 in Berlin. Now there is disillusionment everywhere. All the more should all those who loved her, celebrate her immortality by protecting the world in her spirit, the spirit of her wonderful mind, and liberating it to true freedom.

Beloved Amelia, you will be with us forever, and we with you!

Helga Zepp-LaRouche

This article was translated from German.

Hoover's FBI and Anglo-American Dictatorship

by Anton Chaitkin

In the last article of this series (EIR Aug. 14, 2015), Barbara Boyd explored the methods employed by the FBI and other agencies of the current would-be American police state, and how to combat them effectively, citing the case of Albert Einstein.

In this article, Anton Chaitkin explores the historical emergence of the FBI, and what some have called the modern surveillance state. As Chaitkin demonstrates, this was not some sophisticated plot springing from the head of the monster, J. Edgar Hoover. Rather, its methods and controls were the creation of the British, who, in their preparations for World War I, recruited much of Wall Street directly into the British intelligence services, and went on to establish colonial methods of counterinsurgency as the hegemonic mode of population-control in the United States and elsewhere.

J. Edgar Hoover with his political sponsors, Anglo-American toady presidents Teddy Roosevelt and Woodrow Wilson.

This devolution went through several phases, as the historically direct connection of the United States population to the Constitution, science, and culture was radically transformed. It relied on Wall Street and City of London control over the terrible U.S. Presidents after McKinley's assassination, but it was interrupted by Franklin Delano Roosevelt's recruitment of the population to return to American methods, while condemning and limiting speculative finance. The threatened return of another Roosevelt in the form of the Kennedy Administration, was averted by a wave of assassinations in the 1960s.

This is not some "objective history." When the mafia publicly controlled Las Vegas, in the 1950s and 60s, every gambler was treated as a "mark." After all, why were they in Vegas anyway? What did their very presence say about their morality and sense of principle? Each mark was carefully experimented upon, utilizing various forms of debauchery, sex of every kind and variety, alcohol, and criminal schemes,—all punctuated by the mesmerizing bell which went off every time someone "won" on the slot machines, the same "ding, ding, ding, ding," which opens the New York Stock Exchange every day. As soon as the marks had been stripped of all of their money and their dignity, they were provided a "free" ride home. Broken men and women hanging out in the town was, of course, bad for business.

Director Elia Kazan, who famously ratted out almost all his friends in Hollywood as "Communist sympathizers" in the Hoover-engineered 1950s Red Scare, argued that he had no good choices,—there was only the bad, degenerate choice of cooperating with the Inquisition. In so doing, he merely underlined his cowardice and perfidy. There is a choice, as Einstein showed, as other great leaders who have beaten the British police-state methods have consistently shown. Get smart, be a scientist, explore the weaknesses of this machine, which only works because of popular stupidity and cowardice,—and exploit those weaknesses to create a new republic, just as Alexander Hamilton did.

—The Editors

Part I: The Beginnings

The Wall Street/London coup which gave birth to J. Edgar Hoover and the modern Federal Bureau of Investigation (FBI) completed its first phase in 1901 with the assassination of President William McKinley. The murder of President McKinley would then lead to two disastrous future U.S. Presidencies—those of Theodore ("Teddy") Roosevelt and Woodrow Wilson. Each of these men was raised revering his family's leadership role in the Southern Confederacy, and each was passionately attached to the British aristocracy that had sponsored Southern secession. Both men would be essential to shaping the FBI and the career of J. Edgar Hoover.

Shortly after assuming the Presidency, and with his man William Taft already in Manila, Roosevelt set about transforming the Philippines into America's first colonial venture. Taft's sponsors envisioned Philippine plantations with coolie labor, and Anglo-American imperial adventures on the Asian mainland. With Teddy in the White House, a regime of cruelty and despotism was imposed to crush Filipino resistance as Britain's colonial police did in India and Ireland, and as Emperor Napoleon's secret police had done.

In his history of this tyranny, historian Alfred McCoy told of "five separate secret services ... [with] spies and agents in a ceaseless surveillance of Filipino leaders and their private lives ... media monitoring, psychological profiling ... disinformation, penetration, manipulation ... assassination .... Armed resistance was met with mass slaughter [by] artillery and repeating rifles ...." If they "had something on you," anything humiliating, it could be used to destroy you or turn you into their spy.[1]

This Philippines experiment had a technical manager, a U.S. Army officer named Ralph Van Deman. He systematized surveillance and dirt-collection on every person publicly active in any way in the country. Van Deman's secret service methods enabled efficient government by fear, blackmail, and the disappearance of the troublesome.

President Teddy Roosevelt also connived with Britain to bully Latin America for financiers' debts. He defied Congressional direction to negotiate with Colombia for a canal route through Colombia's province of Panama: a covert Wall Street team ran a fake revolution stealing Panama from Colombia. Oregon's Senator John H. Mitchell attacked the Panama adventure as a House of Morgan swindle.

The President went after Senator Mitchell with a special prosecutor, private detectives, and the Treasury Department's Secret Service. The Senator and scores of

---

1. Alfred McCoy, *Policing America's Empire: The United States, the Philippines, and the Rise of the Surveillance State* (Madison: University of Wisconsin Press, 2009), p. 29.

his political allies were indicted for "land frauds," with the system of spies, perjury, and blackmail being tried out in the Philippines. Mitchell was convicted, defamed in the press, and died before he could appeal.

Teddy Roosevelt now moved to create a permanent national secret police.

He made Charles Bonaparte his Attorney General in 1906: Charles was Emperor Napoleon Bonaparte's great nephew, an Anglophile High Society prince, an admirer of lynching and police shootings. Bonaparte told Congress that the Department of Justice must be given "a force of permanent police … under its control." The idea was to put the Treasury Department's Secret Service (mandated only to guard the currency and protect the President) into use for general domestic espionage.

Anton Chaitkin

Sleepy Hollow Country Club, site of British operative Claude Dansey's intrigues with Wall Street 1911-1914.

Amidst great fear, Congress resisted. Kentucky Democrat Joseph S. Sherley said, "an instrument so dangerous should never be given to an executive unless safeguarded in every way against abuse … [as] a spy system." America's Constitution is not "a system of spying on men and prying into what would ordinarily be designated as their private affairs, to determine whether or not a crime has been committed …."[2] Teddy replied that interference by Congress "will benefit only one class of people—and that is the criminal class … there is no more foolish outcry than this against 'spies'; only criminals need fear our detectives."[3]

The Congress voted May 27, 1908 to prohibit the use of the Treasury Department's Secret Service men as police by the Justice or any other department. Roosevelt sneered that it was "of benefit only to the criminal classes …. The chief argument in favor of the provision was that the Congressmen did not themselves wish to be investigated by Secret Service men."[4] Iowa Republican Walter Smith responded, hitting both Bonaparte's family record and British imperial crimes: "In a free country, no general system of spying upon and espionage of the people, such as has prevailed in Russia, in France under the empire, and at one time in Ireland, should be allowed to grow up …."[5]

Straining under the Congressional restriction, Bonaparte, on Teddy Roosevelt's instructions, created a small investigative agency within the Department of Justice. It was soon thereafter called the *Bureau of Investigation* (in 1935, the name would be changed to the *Federal Bureau of Investigation*).

But this instrument was insufficient for its intended purpose, and the climate did not then exist for its effective use to suppress opposition to the Anglo-American dictatorship.

Part II: An American Secret Police

The British Secret Service in Sleepy Hollow

Beginning in 1909, the British King Edward VII, together with his Secretary of State for War Richard Haldane, began restructuring British intelligence, making two branches of the official secret service later

2. April 1908 Hearings before Subcommittee of House Committee on Appropriations, Sundry Civil Appropriation Bill for 1910 (Washington, D.C.: United States Government Printing Office, 1909.
3. Theodore Roosevelt Letter to House Speaker Joseph Cannon, April 30, 1908, quoted by Roosevelt himself in his Jan. 4, 1909 Special Message to Congress.

4. Jan. 4, 1909 Roosevelt Special Message.
5. Aaron Stockham, "Lack of Oversight: The Relationship Between Congress and the FBI, 1907-1975" (2011). Paper 111.

called MI5 (domestic/counterintelligence) and MI6 (foreign). Beginning in 1910, the new Home Secretary, Winston Churchill, arranged great new powers of surveillance for the secret service, a "registry" of subversives and the clandestine interception of private mail; he put through Parliament a drastic new Official Secrets Act, and recommended passage of a eugenical sterilization law to save the war-destined Empire the expenses of caring for the "unfit."

America itself was the prize to be captured in the planned war.

To coordinate this mission inside the United States, the British secret service assigned Claude Dansey, then a veteran 34-year-old intelligence officer. Dansey had been spy and soldier in Africa and Borneo, and had befriended Winston Churchill in the Boer War.

Claude Dansey first met in the Congo with a syndicate of American oligarchs who had invested capital in support of Belgian King Leopold's slave-labor rubber plantation schemes. Among this group's leaders was Nelson Aldrich, the most powerful U.S. Senator, father-in-law of John D. Rockefeller Jr. and intimate of J.P. Morgan.

In the Autumn of 1911, Captain Dansey took up the full-time position of Resident Secretary of the Sleepy Hollow Country Club, on the Hudson River above New York City. The Rockefeller family had bought this palatial property in 1910 and had created the Club the next year. The Club's chairman was Frank Vanderlip, president of the Rockefellers/Stillman National City Bank, and he had brought Dansey in from the start.

Sleepy Hollow membership was beyond exclusive: Rockefellers and their partners, Morgan men, other ultra-rich friends, including partners in the Aldrich syndicate such as Thomas F. Ryan and Harry Payne Whitney, the latter an heir to Standard Oil. Dansey was particularly close to Ryan and the Whitneys, who had power in the Democratic Party.

Captain Dansey was revered by Club members as a real English gentleman, being above their rank as the descendant of a Duke. As a British secret agent inside America, Dansey ran the spy apparatus that Sir Robert Anderson of Scotland Yard's Special Branch had built up in the late Nineteenth Century against Irish-Americans and other anti-British U.S. citizens.

Then, in November 1912, the Democrat Woodrow Wilson was elected U.S. President.

Wilson immediately stripped Black government employees of all rights and imposed strict racial segregation in Washington. Claude Dansey was in the Administration as *éminence grise* to Wilson's political manager, Edward House, English-educated son of a British Confederate blockade-runner into Texas, and now political boss of Texas.

Nelson Aldrich's Federal Reserve Act and Income Tax Amendment passed Congress in 1913.

Claude Dansey left Sleepy Hollow in mid-1914, returning London to work at British Intelligence headquarters. A few weeks later, World War I broke out in Europe.

A clamor arose among American Anglophiles for the United States to join England in the conflict. In September 1914, one month after Britain declared war, *The New Republic* published its first issue as an American propaganda organ for an Anglo-American alliance. Dorothy Whitney, sister of Congo syndicate member Harry Payne Whitney, and her husband Willard Straight, a Morgan partner working under Sleepy Hollow's Henry Davidson, had launched the magazine based on the cold precepts of H.G. Wells. They made Walter Lippmann, a slavish Wells follower, the editor.

War and Inquisition

Upon America's entry in World War I, Claude Dansey came to Washington, D.C. on behalf of British intelligence and adopted Ralph Van Deman as his understudy. He explained the organization and operation of British intelligence to the awe-struck Anglophile—but not, of course, how the British penetrate the leadership of foreign nations such as America, but how Anglo-Saxon rulers police their population.

Years later, Van Deman proposed that the United States should award his mentor Claude Dansey the Distinguished Service Medal, for guiding the planning and implementation of an American intelligence service. Dansey had a desk in Van Deman's office, "where he could be in touch with everything that was going on. As the Intelligence Section grew and began to take shape, Dansey was called on to give lectures to them, and to the General Staff, lectures which took place behind locked doors guarded by armed soldiers."[6]

America's military leaders had not been interested in Van Deman's plans until Claude Dansey moved into Washington. According to his British biographers, Dansey put his Sleepy Hollow "rolodex" to good use:

"His contacts from those years ... controlled banks

---

6. Anthony Read and David Fisher, *Colonel Z: The Life and Times of a Master of Spies* (London: Hodder and Stoughton, 1984), p. 109.

and railroads in public utilities, as well as production of vital material such as rubber, copper and oil. They were also able to pull strings for him and gain him access to men of power such as Secretary of War [Newton] Baker" to put the plan through.[7]

Ralph Van Deman thus became the boss of a secret police, and, as we shall see, this intrusion into American life would be immediately extended to include the Bureau of Investigation and J. Edgar Hoover. Van Deman and his Philippines-veteran staff went into furious action for the short period the United States would be in the European war. They worked up a "suspect list" consisting of "many hundreds of thousands" of cards on Americans, as had been done earlier in the Philippines.[8]

British Intelligence officer Claude Dansey, who designed America's secret police.

The prime suspects were German-Americans, Irish-Americans, those tied to India, Blacks, immigrants— all considered surveillance-worthy because they were perceived to have a reason to be disloyal to the Anglo-American cause.

This was the madness of war and revenge, when the mass mind can become less than human, and manipulable. With the newspapers (many Wall Street-controlled and under wartime censorship) and the government inducing fear and xenophobia, a vast private army of vigilante spies called the American Protective League (APL) was created while Dansey was instructing Van Deman in the first weeks the United States was in the war.

By arrangement with the Justice Department, Van Deman's Military Intelligence Division (MID) officers directly supervised the civilian APL in coordination with DOJ's tiny Bureau of Investigation. The APL's 350,000 members became official government agents, as the APL badges had it, "Auxiliary to the U.S. Department of Justice."

APL operatives—zealots, cranks, those with private grudges—did millions of investigations, raids, and arrests, and filed 400,000 reports to the government, in a hysterical climate. Guided locally by bankers or corporate officers, they targeted labor organizers and all dissidents. Since predatory trusts had seized the main industries, had destroyed labor relations, and provoked class warfare, Wall Street welcomed the crackdown.

But how was Wall Street involved?

Again, the British biographers fill us in: "At Dansey's suggestion, and initially with his personal help, Van Deman and his people made contact with the efficient information and intelligence departments of the large banks such as National City Bank (in whose board room Dansey had been appointed Resident Secretary of the Sleepy Hollow Country Club and with whose directors he was on intimate terms), and J.P. Morgan and Company (with whom he had close connections through Ryan), and with large corporations such as the Standard Oil companies and the United States Steel Corporation. The success of the scheme depended largely on the confidence which the directors of the corporations concerned had in the military intelligence chiefs and it was invaluable for Van Deman and his successor, General Marlborough Churchill (a very distant American relative of Winston), to have someone like Claude Dansey to help establish personal contact. By the end of the war, virtually every organization with branch offices in the U.S. and abroad was involved."[9]

In the midst of this horrible devolution of Constitutional government, the 22-year-old **J. Edgar Hoover** was first recruited (1917). Just out of law school, he was put in charge of the Department of Justice's War Emergency Division's Enemy Alien Bureau. Immersed in the wildly lawless wartime counterinsurgency, Hoover thus began working with Ralph Van Deman in a partnership that was to last for 35 years, until Van Deman's death.

---

7. *Ibid.* p. 103.

8. Alfred W. McCoy, *op. cit*, p. 299 .

9. Reed and Fisher, *op. cit.* p. 109. Dansey would go on to become de facto head of MI6 for decades into World War Two, through his control of files and of all movements in and out of Britain.

The Birth of Fascism

In February 1919, President Wilson appointed A. Mitchell Palmer as Attorney General. Palmer had been Alien Property Custodian through the war, coordinating with the young J. Edgar Hoover. National strikes loomed in the steel mills and coal mines, and Attorney General Palmer created a General Intelligence (or "Radical") Division in the Bureau of Investigation, and appointed Hoover its head. Military Intelligence and Hoover's agents working together as a single secret service now built up a network of civilian vigilante spies, informers and provocateurs.

With former MID chief Van Deman back in Washington to advise him, Hoover compiled 200,000 cards on "subversives," precisely as Van Deman had done in the Philippines. The wartime American Protective League had been formally dissolved, but the MID/Bureau team put it back into action in various guises.

President Wilson had revived the Ku Klux Klan in 1915 with a White House pre-screening and endorsement of D.W. Griffith's sensational Klan propaganda "Birth of a Nation," a film based on Wilson's own pro-Klan writings and on those of Wilson's close friend Thomas Dixon. After the war, Southern APL members suddenly flooded into the government-approved movement, and it was quickly spread northward.

The MID-Bureau team recruited returning war veterans into the American Legion. After Lt. Col. Theodore Roosevelt, Jr. had convened its start-up conference in St. Louis in May 1919, the Legion was built as the main adjunct to the Federal secret police, growing to over a million members by the end of the year. The Legion, directed by Military Intelligence Chicago station chief Major Thomas Crockett, who had activated covert APL operations across the country, sacked Midwestern political offices. All dissent, any militancy by labor or Blacks, was attributed to the influence of the Russian Bolsheviks or other "reds."

EIRNS/Stuart Lewis

Hoover's Southern Scottish Rite "brother," Klan founder Albert Pike, still has a prominent statue in Washington, D.C.

These auxiliaries were now set loose in the "Palmer Raids," an orgiastic war on unions, radicals, civil rights advocates, teachers, and immigrants from November 1919 to January 1920. This initial descent into a police state was, however, deeply opposed by the American population, and sparked popular protests and outrage.

In 1921, incoming President Warren Harding sought to end wartime emergency government. Detective William J. Burns became Bureau of Investigation Director and cut the number of agents in half.

Part III: Hoover as The Seat of Government

What Was Hoover?

J. Edgar Hoover was peculiarly fitted, as Palmer's deputy, to supervise political mass arrests, deportations, lynchings, terror propaganda, and witch-hunts.

He was a grotesquely deformed personality. His father died of depression in 1921 after years of paranoia, breakdowns, and institutionalizations. J. Edgar continued living alone with his fiercely domineering mother in the Washington, D.C house where he was born, until her death in 1938 when he was 43 years old.

As a youth, he gloried in the revived militant rule of the Southern White Man. Beginning George Washington University in 1913, just as President Wilson had segregated the capital city, he got active in the Kappa Alpha Order.

While organizing the Red Scare of 1919, Hoover was treasurer of the Kappa Alpha's Washington, D.C. chapter.

The Order was founded in Virginia after the Civil War, and spread through the South as a campus companion to the Ku Klux Klan nightriders. It pronounced its spiritual affinity with Robert E. Lee, the Confederate Gentleman. But Kappa Alpha Order shared with the Klan its rituals, ranks, and organizational roots in the

Anglo-American secret world of Southern Scottish Rite Masonry.[10]

Hoover surrounded himself with Southern White Masons in the Kappa Alpha tradition. They were his highest subordinate officers. Hoover himself was raised a Master Mason on November 9, 1920, in Federal Lodge No. 1. He would put a Southern White Masonic unit inside the Bureau itself, called the Fidelity Chapter. He would insist that his agents refer to the Bureau, and his office, as The Seat of Government.

The Southern Scottish Rite moved its headquarters from South Carolina to Washington in 1901, to better carry out its responsibilities in governing the new American empire in the Philippines. Just when the bullet put Teddy Roosevelt in the White House, they put up in Judiciary Square a giant statue honoring its legendary leader, Secession conspirator and Confederate general and Klan founder Albert Pike. J. Edgar Hoover was rising in the secret police under Woodrow Wilson in 1918, when Harper and Brothers published a new edition of President Wilson's *History of the American People*. On page 286, which features photos and drawings of the founding post-Civil War Ku Klux Klan leaders as icons and heroes, Albert Pike is the largest picture, in the center in his full Scottish Rite regalia, and billed as the Klan's "Chief Judicial Officer."

Albert Pike is buried in the wall at the Scottish Rite House of the Temple in Washington; alongside is a complete mockup of J. Edgar Hoover's office and memorabilia, celebrating the most significant Twentieth Century Scottish Rite leader in the Albert Pike tradition.

The Call for Dictatorship

From the beginning of the first World War, *New Republic* editor Walter Lippmann had commanded America to impose a military draft and go to war, while he planned a post-war Wellsian world order. He was commissioned a Captain, and assigned to Intelligence in France under the direction of Edward House. Ralph Van Deman later explained how Lippmann fit in.

Van Deman had come to Paris from London with Claude Dansey on October 2, 1918.

The next morning Captain Walter Lippmann came to the office ... and I had a talk with him concerning propaganda ... On October 5th, Walter Lippmann came in to tell me that he had seen Secretary Baker ... and that I was to take up the propaganda matter with General McAndrews, Chief of Staff, AEF. Colonel Dansey and the British Military Control Officer from Belgrade came in and after luncheon we discussed intelligence matters ....[11]

In 1922, Lippmann called for a dictatorship over the United States to replace the Constitutional system, in his book *Public Opinion*.

Lippmann proclaimed the general public incapable of exercising reasoned judgment. They can think only in "stereotypes" so they believe falsely in "villains and conspiracies. If prices go up unmercifully the profiteers have conspired; if newspapers misrepresent the news, there is a capitalist plot; if the rich are too rich, they have been stealing ...."[12] These dangerous conspiracy theories he then conflates with the every kind of right-wing notion such as Negro self-assertion, short skirts being Communist, and Catholic, Jewish, Japanese, or Masonic plots.

To overcome such ignorance, consent must be engineered by an elite class of experts, using "propaganda." They are to be employed as a professional intelligence corps which will guide the national government from within its every department. This intelligence dictatorship will be permanent, and appointed, not elected, to serve for life.

When the House of Morgan's U.S. Attorney General Harlan Fiske Stone elevated J. Edgar Hoover to head the Bureau in 1924, Stone did not want to repeat the hysterical atmosphere of the Palmer Raids. The explosive public response to the outrages forced a redirection, a more guarded approach. The new Director would exactly fulfill Lippmann's call for "efficient" control of public opinion.

Hoover was a bulldog. He had no female connection beyond his mother, and no real friends. While studying for his law degrees, he had done night-shifts at the Library of Congress, filing and painstakingly compiling

---

10. Officers of the British army occupying the South during the American Revolution, and Americans loyal to the Crown, established the Scottish Rite inside America, countering the Masonic faction of Franklin, Washington and Lafayette. See Anton Chaitkin, *Treason in America, from Aaron Burr to Averell Harriman* (Kindle edition), chapter 10.

11. Ralph Van Deman, *The Final Memorandum* (Wilmington: Scholarly Resources, 1988), p. 72.

12. Walter Lippmann, *Public Opinion* (New York: Harcourt, Brace and Company, 1922) pp. 128-129.

British viceroys John D. Rockefeller and John D. Rockefeller Jr., who, along with J.P. Morgan, put J. Edgar Hoover in power.

Library of Congress

information in categories. He had a steel-trap memory for details that might be used as weapons. At the Bureau he worked all the time, and demanded his subordinates do the same.

He venerated authority, knowing nothing of principles that should justify it. He proved he would do absolutely anything, quietly destroy or kill, to defend the power of those who sponsored him. This reverence began with Harlan Stone, Rockefeller, Morgan, British gentlemen, his "betters." It went on to cruder sorts with deep pockets for him, the Texas fascist oligarchs Clint Murchison, Sid Richardson, and H.L. Hunt. In the British imperial tradition, he was excited to use the ugliest and most lawless methods, in a universe of insider secrets, to preserve what was respected. This allowed free association with organized crime while publicly denying its very existence.

The appointment was effectively for life, as

Lippmann had specified for the intelligence dictatorship. Hoover's cunning sense of political winds, his attachment of the Bureau to the British Secret Intelligence Service, and to those U.S. military elements compatible with his views, allowed him to gather and hold power for half a century.

'Professionals'

Attorney General Harlan Stone instructed Hoover that he was to remodel the Bureau on the lines of Britain's **Scotland Yard**, for efficiency.

For public acceptance, a national secret police must be "professional." Under Hoover, the Bureau brought in whatever was up-to-date in "forensics."

The use of unique individual **fingerprints** for identification was first developed by the British Imperial administration in India. Sir William Herschel studied the phenomenon for 20 years before applying it to the management of prisoners in Bengal in the 1870s. The subject was taken up, at Charles Darwin's suggestion, by his cousin Francis Galton as a companion to Galton's invention of "eugenics"—the science of perpetuating the better people by the destruction of the weaker. Galton's 1892 book, *Finger Prints*, was the definitive introduction of the matter to the attention of governments. The Empire established a Fingerprint Bureau in Calcutta in 1898, and within Scotland Yard in 1901.

French police officer Alphonse Bertillon developed the science of **anthropometry,** the use of bodily measurements in analyzing crime. Bertillon's expert testimony in the famous Dreyfus case contributed greatly to the wrongful conviction, with his dubious science masking anti-Semitism and anti-German warmongering. Bertillon inspired Arthur Conan Doyle for his Sherlock Holmes detective stories.

The Bureau expended considerable resources advertizing its effective use of these laboratory tools. The fact that Hoover's reign coincided with a sensational outburst of crime in the United States—syndicate gangsterism, audacious Wall Street looting schemes, mass lynching of Blacks, the Ku Klux Klan marching in Washington and the Midwest—did not seem to diminish public faith in the Professionalism of the Bureau's methods.

J. Edgar Hoover's agents constructed a nationwide grid of thousands of informers, spies, and criminals. An individual would be leaned on and "turned" to the Bureau's use; this was the case with many homosexuals, blackmailed through fear of exposure.

Hoover used the threat of his secret files to blackmail Congress into submission, extracting constantly expanding budgets. He gained influence within every department of the Federal government, and leveraging the hand of the Bureau in local police departments, within local and state governments as well.

From the 1920s onward, Bureau agents visited colleges and book publishers, coercing them to silence or purge dissenters. Direct Bureau pressure on newspapers, for censorship and to publish Hoover's stream of propaganda, combined with increasing Wall Street ownership to form a media cartel as effective as any overt tyrant could construct.

In 1928 Edward Bernays' book *Propaganda* celebrated the success of his own class of Wall Street-paid opinion molders:

> The conscious and intelligent manipulation of the organized habits and opinions of the masses is an important element in democratic society. Those who manipulate this unseen mechanism of society constitute an invisible government which is the true ruling power of our country … It is not usually recognized how necessary these invisible governors are to the orderly functioning of our group life…[13]

Part IV: FDR Takes Charge

By the end of the 1920s, the hurricane of crime by London and Wall Street had obliterated the world economy. When the Great Depression hit, Hoover blamed the general lawlessness on inefficient, corrupt local politicians and police. Power to the Bureau was the solution.

The Headline: "American Crime Records Found of Little Use." The story: "The Bureau of Investigation … under J. Edgar Hoover … has been actively preparing for the collection of [local] police crime records … and will … [be] taking over the work … which has previously been done by the International Association of Chiefs of Police, with the aid of the Rockefeller Foundation. [The IACP and the Rockefellers asked for Hoover to take over and this was] authorized … by a law passed in the last Congress."[14]

Hoover told Congress why Depression-ruined communities were restless: "The Communist Party … has organized a … committee to incite revolutionary activities among the Negroes and to send selected Negroes to Moscow for … communistic training for world revolution …. [The communists] stirred up discontent among the unemployed American wage earners …."[15]

Yet the global collapse opened up the possibility that new leadership might reverse the destruction of human society.

Franklin Roosevelt had changed deeply since his role as Assistant Navy Secretary in the Wilson Administration's wartime and post-war actions.

While recovering from polio beginning in 1921, FDR found a passion for America's founding mission and assessed the Anglo-American financiers as the nation's lethal enemy.[16] Aware of his opponents' astonishingly evil intentions, he assembled a political machine to recover American sovereign power.

War at the Outset

A potential large popular majority backed Roosevelt's strategic turn, but he first had to prevail in a bloody struggle.

He broke the dominance of the Morgan-run Democratic Party leaders and installed his close friend Thomas J. Walsh as the 1932 Democratic convention chairman.

Montana Senator Walsh "knew where the bodies were buried."

Thomas Walsh had led the battle at the 1921 Senate hearings on the Justice Department's illegal practices. There he confronted Palmer and his deputy Hoover with evidence they had perpetrated "an orgy of terror, violence and crime against citizens and aliens…." Under Walsh's questioning, Hoover told him the Justice Dept. had suffered under the Constitutional "handicap" that immigrants were entitled to have lawyers, and had changed "Rule 22" to eliminate that right.

Hoover had to burn quietly as Walsh introduced a confidential memo sent to a Boston Bureau agent December 27, 1919:

13. Edward Bernays, *Propaganda* (New York: H. Liveright, 1928), p. 1.
14. *Christian Science Monitor*, August 29, 1930, p. 3.

15. *Washington Post*, June 11, 1930, p. 1.
16. He attacked the Panama actions of his cousin Teddy Roosevelt and the "sterile" Dollar Diplomacy policy that had brought us "fear and ridicule," as a betrayal of our Revolutionary heritage; see FDR's "Our Foreign Policy, A Democratic View," *Foreign Affairs*, July 1928.

If possible you should arrange with your undercover informants to have meetings of the Communist Party and the Communist Labor Party held on the night set. I have been informed by some of the bureau officers that such arrangements will be made. This, of course, would facilitate the making of the arrests. On the evening of the arrests, this office will be open the entire night, and I desire that you communicate by long distance [telephone] to Mr. Hoover any matters of importance (during the course of the arrests ....[17]

Walsh remained in the Senate as J. Edgar Hoover's dedicated enemy.

After Senator Walsh had presided over his Presidential nomination victory, Roosevelt rallied previously hopeless millions by speaking out as others feared to do. He directly assailed the predators who had to be displaced from power:

We find two-thirds of American industry concentrated in a few hundred corporations, and actually managed by not more than five human individuals ... fewer than three dozen private banking houses, and stock-selling adjuncts of commercial banks, directing the flow of American capital .... [The] Government, without becoming a prying bureaucracy, can act as a check or counterbalance to this oligarchy so as to secure the chance to work and the safety of savings to men and women, rather than ... safety of

FDR's Attorney General designee Thomas J. Walsh, who died shockingly after announcing he would clean out the DOJ.

manipulation to the financial manipulators ....[18]

Roosevelt won the election November 8, 1932; he was to take office in March.

On February 15, 1933, an assassin shot at President-elect Roosevelt; but the shot hit and killed a member of FDR's entourage, Chicago Mayor Anton Cermak.

On February 26, Roosevelt made it known he would appoint Senator Thomas J. Walsh as U.S. Attorney General.

On March 1, the *New York Times* reported Walsh's pledge that "he would re-organize the Department of Justice when he assumes office, probably with an almost completely new personnel."[19]

Walsh was found dead the next morning, while on a train to Washington, D.C. for Roosevelt's March 4 inauguration and his own swearing-in.

Senator Walsh's son-in-law, Navy Captain Emmett C. Gudger, believing Walsh had been poisoned, insisted on an autopsy. When that was refused, Gudger tried unsuccessfully to have the body exhumed. A Bureau agent had been on the death train, and when Director Hoover personally met the train on arrival in Washington, that agent gave him a complete account. Stunned by Walsh's sudden death, FDR took no action to displace J. Edgar Hoover.

That July 1933, and the following Spring 1934, American Legion officials paid by Morgan's men asked Marine Corps General Smedley Butler to lead a *coup d'état* against President Roosevelt, based on their study of how European fascists had used veterans to seize power. When the plot to overthrow the government hit the headlines, General Butler went to J. Edgar Hoover for action. Hoover refused: there was no evidence a federal criminal statute had been violated.

17. Hearings of the Judiciary Committee's Subcommittee on Charges of Illegal Practices of the Department of Justice, January 19-March 3, 1921; memo on page 14. A Boston Federal court had already ruled in June, 1920 that the Palmer Justice Department had itself created radical units. Judge George W. Anderson stated, "What does appear, beyond reasonable doubt, is that the Government owns and operates some part of the Communist Party."

18. Campaign Address at Columbus, Ohio, Aug. 20, 1932.
19. *New York Times*, March 1, 1933, p. 2.

'The President Authorized It'

Although J. Edgar Hoover's publicity machine pumped him as the scourge of bank robbers and kidnappers, he never felt safe openly challenging FDR. Historians have generally received without question Hoover's own dubious accounts of their relationship. For example: He met with FDR August 24, 1936, and then claimed that Roosevelt had asked him to investigate "subversives"—i.e., had authorized his unlimited power to hunt for fascists, but especially communists. This passed into accepted history.

Hoover had just previously won a round in his power struggle with the Administration. One newspaper report read:

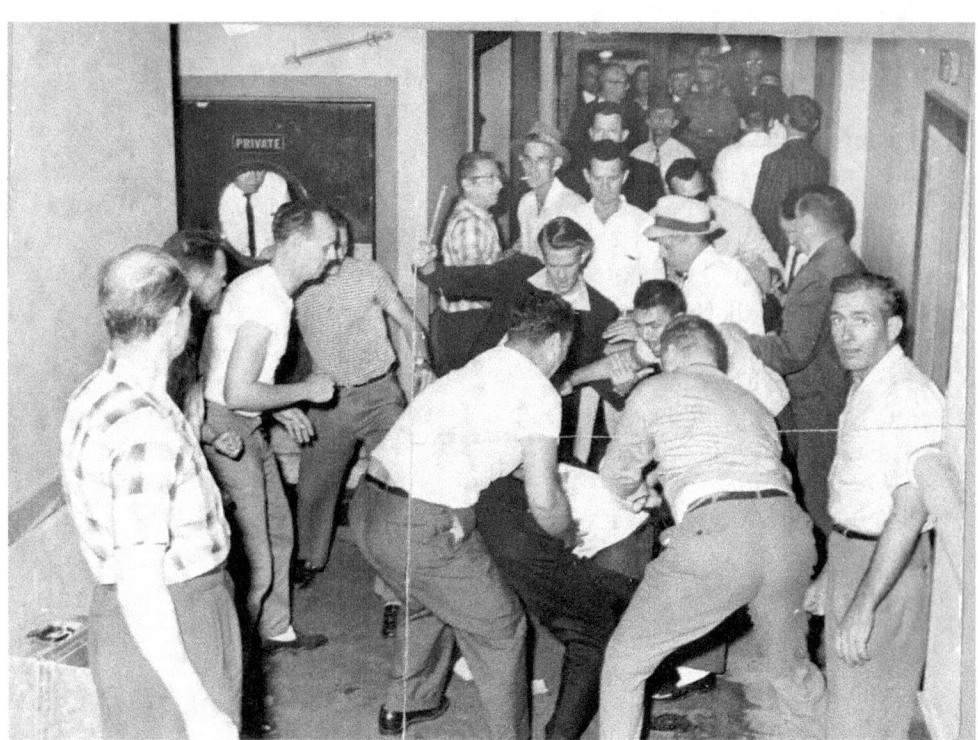
Federal Bureau of Investigation

Freedom Riders being beaten by Klan gangs coordinated by J. Edgar Hoover.

> Departmental jealousy roused by the meteoric rise of J. Edgar Hoover ... came out into the open today as two Secret Service men of the Treasury Department were demoted for allegedly spying on G-men [FBI] activities .... The situation is likely to have a far-reaching reaction, with the smoldering opposition to Mr. Hoover coming to the front from certain elements who admire him as an executive, but believe his personal publicity should be curbed. The late Senator Thomas J. Walsh, selected by Mr. Roosevelt originally for Attorney General, for example, is said to have declared that one of his first acts would be to oust J. Edgar Hoover.[20]

Treasury Secretary Henry Morgenthau had sought to slow down Hoover's well-connected power grab. He was outmaneuvered and had to apologize.

As World War II broke out in Europe, President Roosevelt asked citizens and police to report sabotage

---

20. *Christian Science Monitor*, August 6, 1936, "G-Man Hoover Wins His Fight on Espionage ... Morgenthau Regrets," p. 1.

or espionage to the FBI. Hoover on his own initiative, under cover of these orders, formed a Custodial Detention Index, detailing all persons who should be subject to arrest in case of emergency. American Civil Liberties Director Roger Baldwin was on the list. In mid-1943, long after the United States had entered the war, Attorney General Francis Biddle ordered Hoover to abolish the secret list. Hoover changed its name to Security Index and continued to maintain it.

Hoover's Targets

A review of J. Edgar Hoover's most important enemies in the Roosevelt era will offer a preview of his part in the betrayal of the country after FDR's death.

Medal of Honor winner Colonel William J. Donovan first ran up against Hoover in 1924, when he was his immediate superior in the Justice Department. Donovan saw what Hoover was and soon asked for him to be fired. He had then tried to stop Harlan Stone from making Hoover the Director. Incoming President Herbert Hoover (no relation to J. Edgar) considered appointing Donovan Attorney General in 1929; Director Hoover ran the covert campaign that aborted the nomination.

FDR had to navigate treacherous waters in preparing the country to deal with the ongoing war between Britain, whose Empire he despised, and the fascist Axis, which that Empire had promoted and built up against Russia. Roosevelt began shaping a U.S. intelligence capability under the President's centralized control, to be guided by Colonel Donovan. From 1941 to the end of the war, J. Edgar Hoover used every available weapon to sabotage Donovan and to preserve his own pre-eminence. Britain officially coordinated with Donovan and his Office of Strategic Services, but increasingly teamed with Hoover to target their mutual enemies, and thus pre-determine the shape of the postwar world.

Hoover's FBI carried out a long war to discredit and deport Albert Einstein, a refugee from likely death in Hitler-plagued Europe. Britain's science elite loathed him as the man who had shattered their dead-universe doctrine. It was Einstein who had alerted President Roosevelt to the danger of Nazi Germany's possible development of an atomic bomb. But Hoover's covert circulation of "subversive" slanders led the Army to block Einstein himself from participating in the U.S. bomb program, the Manhattan Project.

Treasury official Harry Dexter White began formulating FDR's plans for a prosperous postwar world before the United States entered the war. White designed the World Bank and International Monetary Fund to be instruments in lifting poor nations into modern times, thereby securing peace. J. Edgar Hoover built up files against White and pressed for his removal on the bogus charge he was a communist. Britain's ambassador Lord Halifax visited Roosevelt to claim White was a Russian agent. Knowing Halifax had led Britain's efforts to build up Hitler's power, FDR showed him the door.

Hoover campaigned covertly against Vice President Henry Wallace, shadowed him everywhere, and planted gossip, to prevent him from seeking his re-election with FDR in 1944. Finally, powerbroker Charles Marsh, an oilman in the circles of Hoover's Texas patrons and an avid agent of the British Foreign Office, hosted a party with Wallace where British agents were able to steal a copy of Wallace's draft pamphlet, outlining the Administration's plans to dismantle Britain's Asian empire. The pamphlet was sent to Winston Churchill, and the British and Hoover thereafter used their American political assets to force Wallace off the 1944 ticket.

Thus it was Harry Truman who succeeded FDR in 1945, not Wallace. Truman invited Winston Churchill to define America's policy as a Cold War—permanent war—and the merger of American and British strategic agencies.

Intelligence agents loyal to Roosevelt's outlook were immediately sacked after his death. William Donovan made a bid to be appointed head of the new Central Intelligence Agency, but Hoover moved successfully to block him, and boasted about it to the end of his life.

After Harry Dexter White was appointed executive director of the International Monetary fund, J. Edgar Hoover bullied Truman until White was forced to resign. The IMF became a coercive device for impoverishment rather than a tool for progress.

J. Edgar Hoover had helped bring about a new order with an expanded "intelligence community" around Allen Dulles, the British royal family's Round Table faction and its Wall Street partners.

There was a division of labor. The FBI fed witch-hunts by Congressional committees, by President Truman, by Senator Joseph R. McCarthy, and by the young California Congressman Richard M. Nixon. The CIA and British Intelligence jointly overthrew foreign democratic governments, promoted ugliness and banality in the arts, and pushed a drug culture.

The criminal Mafia came to be an extension of both FBI and CIA. Both deployed Cuban émigré terrorists, and a military faction with a hatred of American ideals was on the Dulles-Hoover team. CIA and FBI shared ownership of American leftist movements, castrating them, and both agencies ran counter-gangs against real dissenters.

Both CIA and FBI engaged full-time in falsifying history, an absolute requirement for success in perpetrating the biggest crimes.

This has often been quite crude.

Henry Morgenthau, Jr., Treasury Secretary from 1934 to 1945, kept a detailed daily diary as an insider in the Roosevelt Administration. He gave his papers to the National Archives, and in 1951 was talking of publishing the diaries.

The leader of the FBI team that Hoover dispatched to handle this problem later gave this narrative to Hoover biographer Curt Gentry:

"... There were five of us, and we were all sworn to absolute secrecy. We even left the Washington field office by various devious routes. And we'd go in at different times so no one [at the National Archives] would know five agents were in that room. And we were the only ones who had a key .... We literally went through [the diary] with scissors, cutting out any references which would be unfavorable to Mr. Hoover or the FBI ...." The pages were then re-typed and renumbered so that there would be no indication that anything was missing .... What they left behind for the historians who followed was a history of the New Deal years as approved by J. Edgar Hoover.[21]

White House photo office

Warren Commission delivers its report. Congressman Hale Boggs (on the right) saw its fraud, sparked a real prosecution, and denounced Hoover's Gestapo.

Part V: Treason as the Deepest Moral Challenge

Following Franklin Roosevelt's death, America was to be purged of the Revolutionary moral qualities thought dangerous by the ruling London-Wall Street axis. Hoover's FBI supplied all the fuel for the Inquisition's fire.

Soviet Russia and the states it ruled in divided Europe suffered under Communist secret police regimes, a fact recognized by patriots and transnational oligarchs alike. Here was the background and pretext for the nightmare induced by Hoover and his clients.

Betrayal was their strategy: under terror of denunciation, a man would betray himself and his friends, would falsely confess or falsely accuse to escape the fire. After all, wasn't there a great deal of truth in what the interrogator said about the Soviets? Few souls were great enough to point to the historic betrayal of the United States that was before everyone's eyes.

Albert Einstein's open letter[22] to persecuted teacher William Frauenglass, asking thinkers to *refuse cooperation and go to jail and ruin rather than betray their country*, shamed many and sparked a fight. Hoover's fury was heightened by Einstein's outspoken defense of African Americans fighting racial persecution, a movement just then beginning to grow.

John F. Kennedy entered the Presidency committed to substitute for the Cold War trap a "grand and global alliance, North and South, East and West," against "the common enemies of man: tyranny, poverty, disease, and war itself." Initially paralyzed by the ploys of opposed strategy-makers, Kennedy learned in the White House how he could accomplish the goals he had sought since he had served FDR, his wartime Commander-in-Chief and Presidential model.

He began to restore industry, to pioneer space exploration, to inspire anti-colonial leaders and to offer the Soviets a path for both sides to escape the trap.[23]

The rising Black civil rights movement just then gained unprecedented White support. That this movement and Martin Luther King's leadership could give JFK's Presidency powerful new potential, was conveyed to him by his brother Robert Kennedy—the At-

21. Curt Gentry, *J. Edgar Hoover, The Man and the Secrets* (New York: Norton & Co., 1991), pp. 389-390.
22. *New York Times*, June 12, 1953, p. 1, 9.

23. see Anton Chaitkin, "John F. Kennedy vs. the Empire," *Executive Intelligence Review*, September 6, 2013.

torney General and constitutionally the boss of J. Edgar Hoover, who despised and feared him. John F. Kennedy was shot to death in Dallas, Texas November 22, 1963.

The FBI proclaimed that Lee Harvey Oswald was the killer. Oswald was murdered two days later, before he could be tried. Hoover sent a Justice Department official to Dallas to shut down local police investigation. The FBI scooped up and secreted away evidence about Oswald and his killer, Jack Ruby. President Lyndon Johnson appointed a Commission (including Allen Dulles, whom Kennedy had fired as CIA Director) which certified that nothing had happened except that a lone nut had killed the President.

The old FDR Congressman Hale Boggs of Louisiana was a member of that Warren Commission. Jack Ruby's intelligence agency connections disturbed him; he suspected that Oswald's background had been falsified and records forged.

In 1965 Rep. Boggs told New Orleans District Attorney Jim Garrison that Oswald could not have fired the fatal shots. With Boggs' encouragement, Garrison began the only law enforcement prosecution of the President's murder.

Assassination suspects probed by Garrison had flagrant FBI and CIA backgrounds. Guy Bannister, former Special Agent in Charge of Chicago Office, a reputed assassination planner, and CIA contract pilot David Ferrie together ran Oswald as a patsy. Bannister deployed former FBI agent I.P. Nitschke and three CIA men. Garrison formally charged Clay Shaw, a New Orleans partner in the Dulles-British MI6 joint international joint murder apparatus, as an assassination planner. Justice department attorney Walter Sheridan betrayed Attorney General Robert Kennedy and directed the slanders destroying Garrison's case.

A cyclone of confetti, an industry of conspiracy theories, went up to overawe the simple but terrifying necessity for considering what had happened to the nation, and what must be done about it.

Martin Luther King survived the FBI's long war to destroy him; he did not break when the FBI sent his family a surveillance tape with the demand that he kill himself. When he fought to pull the country out of Vietnam, out of the Anglo-American permanent war policy, he was shot to death. James Earl Ray confessed to avoid execution, then recanted.

Robert Kennedy, the clear favorite to succeed John-son as President, was shot to death while campaigning soon afterwards. Sirhan Sirhan confessed to the murder, but later recanted and said he had no recollection of having confessed.

With the Kennedys and King gone, Richard Nixon took the Presidency.

Hale Boggs called on Nixon's Attorney General John Mitchell to have the courage to fire J. Edgar Hoover. Boggs "accused Mr. Hoover and the bureau of tapping the telephones of members of Congress and of stationing agents on college campuses to spy on students and faculty members. He said these were 'the tactics of the Soviet Union and Hitler's Gestapo.' "[24]

The following year the private airplane carrying Hale Boggs disappeared without a trace. The FBI later subjected Congress to a provocateur witch-hunt called ABSCAM, the members cooperating and implicating each other in fear of their careers.

The nation, and the Congress as an institution, were supine by the time of the terror attacks of September 11, 2001, and have remained in moral paralysis ever since through the evolution of the "anti-terror" chaos.

Now the financial superstructure has dissolved under quadrillions of dollars in speculation. At present, the Anglo-Americans are generating a fast-developing crisis, against and all around Russia, that threatens to devolve into a nuclear war.

China, Russia, India, Brazil, and South Africa (the BRICS nations) have associated as the core for a rescue strategy of vast Twenty-First Century industrial and infrastructure progress. The old British imperial view, governing the United States, is that even the greatest conceivable tragedy is preferable to an overwhelming world majority of Asians and Africans, scientifically and economically advanced and leading world opinion against a de-industrialized West.

The BRICS have asked the United States to join them.

This country was the originator of the inventive and moral conceptions that gave rise to man's greatest power over nature, a power that will save us all if its progress is allowed to resume.

Reflecting on that beautiful legacy, and how it was subdued, will help us decide to fight for its return.

24. *New York Times*, April 6, 1971, "Boggs Demands That Hoover Quit," p. 1.

www.ingramcontent.com/pod-product-compliance
Lightning Source LLC
Chambersburg PA
CBHW081153280526
45787CB00008B/3319